Hope for Hard Times

ALSO BY MAGREY R. DEVEGA:

Awaiting the Already

Embracing the Uncertain

One Faithful Promise

Magrey R. deVega

Hope *for* Hard Times

Lessons on Faith from Elijah and Elisha

Abingdon Press / Nashville

HOPE FOR HARD TIMES
Lessons on Faith from Elijah and Elisha

Library of Congress Cataloging-in-Publication data has been requested.

978-1-5018-8138-1

19 20 21 22 23 24 25 26 27 28—10 9 8 7 6 5 4 3 2 1
MANUFACTURED IN THE UNITED STATES OF AMERICA

To my brothers on the journey:
Brett, Scott, Steve, Roy, David,
Cameron, David, and Craig

To Mike and Nancy

To the faithful disciples of
Hyde Park United Methodist Church

And to my wonderful family,
especially Grace and Madelyn

CONTENTS

INTRODUCTION

We've all been there. Rock bottom. The end of our rope. The last straw. During hard times, it can seem like the only option is to throw in the towel.

But throughout their thirty years of combined ministry, the great biblical prophets Elijah and Elisha offered this consistent message: Don't give up, and don't lose hope. Trust that God will help you find a way.

Just look at what Elijah did for the widow who was down to her last bit of oil and flour. Watch him face down the opposition in a mountaintop showdown. Follow him into the cave when he felt all alone and ready to give up, and listen with him for God's still small voice. Look at Elisha pick up Elijah's mantle and determine to continue his work. Watch Elisha talk to Naaman and bring him a healing he didn't even know he needed. When surrounded by enemies who wanted him dead, watch him pray with eyes opened to hope.

And if you look closely at the stories of Elijah and Elisha from 1 Kings 17 to 2 Kings 8, you'll find your name in there. Your story of hurt, heartache, and hopelessness has been heard, and God has a message for you. There is hope for you in hard times.

Read these stories, pray through them, and listen, as you receive encouragement and guidance for whatever you are facing today. Open your eyes and open your hands. For just like the ravens at the Cherith Brook, God is with you, giving you everything you need.

The following stories are much more than fanciful tales from the past. They are deeply theological meditations on where to find God when hard times hit us. It is hard enough to be confronted by situations that seem overwhelming to us. But what makes them even tougher is when our view of God is challenged—when much of what we thought that we believed about God is called into question.

Many of the following stories may connect directly with a tough situation you are facing today, and some may not. You may find yourself entering some of the narratives more easily than others.

But all of these stories, to some degree, invite you to think about where God is in your life right now and what God is doing. More importantly, these stories will push you to leave room for novelty, for some new way that God is at work that you may not have noticed before.

That is the key to finding hope in hard times, according to Elijah and Elisha.

When the culture around us seems to oppose our belief in God, how do we maintain our convictions? Elijah shows us how at the showdown on Mount Carmel.

When we can't hear God like we might have in the past, where is God to be found? Elijah learns how in a cave on Mount Horeb.

When the reality of our mortality is closing in on our days, and we wonder what impact God can make beyond our years, Elijah and Elisha show us when Elijah passes on his mantle.

When healing doesn't happen in the way we expect, Elisha shows us how to trust in God to find healing in a way we didn't expect, through his conversation with Naaman.

And when we feel surrounded by fear and that God is nowhere to be found, Elisha shows us we can open our eyes to see a God who has been with us all along.

So, Elijah and Elisha are more than prophets from the past or characters from times long gone. They are here today with us, as tour guides in a whole new gallery of God's work and presence in our lives. Let's follow them, and listen as they point out things to us we might have never noticed about God, ourselves, and our relationship to God.

What we will discover is hope. Even amid the hardest times.

Chapter 1

When the Odds Seem Against You

CHAPTER 1
WHEN THE ODDS SEEM AGAINST YOU

Opening the Bible and beginning to read a story can feel a lot like landing in a foreign country without a map. It helps to have some basic orientation to your surroundings and a direction to follow to help you become familiar.

Such is the case for the stories of Elijah and Elisha. Though they are among the better known and most often referenced characters in the Bible, when Elijah enters the scene in 1 Kings 17, we need some background on what was happening around him in order to appreciate his story.

The death of King Solomon ushered in an important change in Israelite history. Up until then, the Israelites had risen from humble beginnings as descendants of Abraham (Genesis), slaves in Egypt, and wandering nomads in the wilderness (Exodus–Deuteronomy). They had entered the Promised Land (Joshua) and carved out an existence as a collection of tribes without much central leadership (Judges). At last, the first kings came to power, which would prove a mixed blessing. Israel had reached the height of military and economic power under King David (1–2 Samuel) and his son Solomon (1 Kings 2–11). These were the glory days of the Israelite empire, often referred to as the era of Zion.

But in the second half of the tenth century BC, around the year 922, King Solomon died. The northern tribes, led by a charismatic leader named Jeroboam, revolted against Solomon's son, Rehoboam. They broke away and became independent; the once-mighty empire split into a northern kingdom called Israel and a southern kingdom called Judah.

There were a number of reasons for the division of the kingdoms; 1 Kings presents this in part as a punishment for Solomon's idolatry later in life, and Jeroboam seemed to be reacting to heavy taxation and conscripted labor. There were also cultural and religious divisions that likely played an important role, including the two kingdoms' understanding of God and the shape of God's intervention in human life.

The people of the Southern Kingdom focused on God's covenant with David, holding on to God's promise to bless the people with land, the Temple, and a continuous lineage of royal rule. David's dynasty persisted throughout the history of the Southern Kingdom. Their kings were selected by heredity, as an ongoing genealogy dating back to King David. Rehoboam, Jehoshaphat,

Uzziah, Manasseh, Josiah, and many others, twenty in all, were all kings of Judah and descendants of David.

This outlook might be understood as one that emphasized God's steadfastness, protection, and ongoing presence. God was reliable and could be trusted, even if God was not quite predictable. God's presence could always be found in the Temple of Jerusalem (where God sat), in the divinely appointed king (through whom God ruled), and in the land (which was a fulfillment of God's ancestral promise). And God could be trusted to protect the people and the land because of the special relationship with the king and the Temple.

In contrast to this more "fixed" view of God in the south, the Israelites in the Northern Kingdom of Israel emphasized a different set of traditions. They focused more on God's deliverance of the Israelites from slavery in Egypt and their wandering in the wilderness, during which time God went with the people. They were therefore less tied to the Temple in Jerusalem or direct lineage to David. They established their capital in Shechem and later Samaria, and they rooted their memory not in the Temple but in the Tabernacle, the mobile worship center that allowed their ancestors to follow God through the wilderness in Exodus.

A key difference between the north and the south was in the way the north chose their kings. In the south the dynasty of David remained strong, and though there were competition and power games, a descendant of David was always on the throne. But in the Northern Kingdom, a single dynasty could not gain a foothold for very long. The people of the north seemed much more open to following leaders based on charisma—that is, evidence that the Spirit of God had rested on a particular person, for a season of time, evidenced by the blessings God had bestowed on the people through their leadership.

And when there was no longer evidence that they were following God's lead, or that God had moved on to someone else? It was time for a new king. And often that led to rebellion, revolt, and even assassination to usher in a new ruler.

So, of the nineteen kings in the north, how many died by assassination? Eight. And of the twenty kings in the south, how many died by assassination? Zero.

Clearly, being a prophet in the Northern Kingdom—the setting for the stories that follow—was deathly business. To discern for the people whether God's Spirit had moved on to another ruler was to live a life fraught with risk.

The Purpose of the Prophets

Prophets were often plucked from obscurity, sometimes with no name recognition or impressive skills, in order to carry out the most dangerous missions. They spoke words of truth against powerful people too hard-hearted to receive them and against populations of people too brittle to respond. Many of these prophets endured long stretches of loneliness, starvation, and fear for their own well-being.

Yet they served one of the most vital roles in the entire Bible. They were God's mouthpieces, offering course corrections for wayward people and wicked rulers. They did so with dazzling demonstrations of power and performance art. They were equal parts street performer, political pundit, operative, and wordsmith.

Their lives serve as examples to us of how to live with courage, integrity, and faith amid dangerous adversaries and troubling times. When the people were more prone to follow their own understanding and their own pathway to power and prosperity, the prophets spoke out. They challenged people to open up their minds and their hearts to new ways of understanding God, of living out God's commands, and of relating to one other—even as they reminded them of God's covenant made with them long ago. They called people to faithfulness, even when the world around them was changing. And they showed people how to see God amid their hard times in a way they never had before.

And most of the time, a prophet had an adversary.

Every good story, after all, needs a villain. Batman had the Joker, the Avengers had Thanos, and Luke Skywalker had the Emperor. Screenwriters and novelists know that what really propels a good story is not the setting or the characters. It's the conflict. Good, juicy, delicious moments of tension suck you in and make you choose sides. Hero or villain? Bully or underdog? Good or evil?

The historian of 1 Kings must have known this, since there is no doubt that when it came to chronicling the adventures of the prophets Elijah and Elisha, the author paid careful attention to their rivals, King Ahab and Queen Jezebel. More words are used to describe the wickedness of these two individuals than are used to describe any other villain in the entire Bible—more than Pharaoh, more than Judas, more than Goliath, more than anyone.

It is clear all throughout these stories who the bad guys are: Ahab and Jezebel exemplified evil.

Ahab was the seventh king of the Northern Kingdom, whose rule started just fifty years after the nation of Israel divided. He succeeded his father, Omri, who ruled briefly until dying of natural causes. In describing the beginning of Ahab's reign, the Bible wastes no time in telling us about his eventual legacy:

> *He ruled over Israel in Samaria for twenty-two years and did evil in the LORD's eyes, more than anyone who preceded him. Ahab found it easy to walk in the sins of Jeroboam, Nebat's son. He married Jezebel the daughter of Ethbaal, who was the king of the Sidonians. He served and worshipped Baal. He made an altar for Baal in the Baal temple he had constructed in Samaria. Ahab also made a sacred pole and did more to anger the LORD, the God of Israel, than any of Israel's kings who preceded him.*
>
> (1 Kings 16:29b-33)

There is no mistaking who the antagonist of this story would be. The people of the Northern Kingdom, who so often needed to discern how well their king was demonstrating the fruit of God's anointing, were now being led by someone who would be the most wayward ruler they would ever know.

The times required a course correction, a messenger with a challenging message, a person who would stand tall and do a most unenviable job. The times required a prophet, a person who would speak God's truth to earthly powers.

The God Who Calls and Provides
1 Kings 17:1-6

We are told very little about Elijah when he is introduced in 1 Kings 17. He was a native of Tishbe, from the region of Gilead, east of the Jordan River, and part of the Northern Kingdom. That's all we know. No lineage, no call story, no special skillsets that made him right for the job. He bursts onto the scene out of nowhere with a formidable mission: tell Ahab that he has stopped following the ways of the Lord.

This is the first of many entry points in the stories of Elijah and Elisha that invite us to identify ourselves in their struggles. If you have ever had the daunting task of speaking a hard truth to someone you know, especially someone you love, you know what an emotionally burdensome job that is.

When you are watching a loved one slowly kill himself, one bottle at a time;

When the employer who holds both your career and your livelihood with one hand is bilking the company behind his back with the other;

When your elected government official is skirting her responsibility, promoting self over common good;

When the ones you trust to do what is right choose expediency over integrity, and the way of power over the way of decency and love;

And when the only person who can challenge them is . . . you.

It's not a task you wanted, and not one you would readily accept. If there were any way for you to shirk that call, to pawn it off on someone else, you would. But you know better. Sometimes the hard job of speaking the truth in love, to someone you love or someone with more power than you have, is the most unenviable job in life.

It's what makes the story of Elijah—and every prophet, really— so endearing and so relevant for us. We would much rather God choose someone else. Our life would be easier, and our days more joyous. But when the times demand it, and we feel the burden of that call is too heavy to avoid, we turn to people like Elijah to follow their example. We push ahead, and we trust that God will be with us, giving us the word and strengthening our every move.

A Wilderness . . . Blessing?

Elijah's first message was simple: There was going to be a long drought, and it wasn't going to end until God said so. Such a drought would be devastating for the people and for the economy, so this news was about as bad as it could get.

And that was just Elijah's first day on the job.

God then told Elijah to go out into the wilderness for a while, to the Cherith Brook (1 Kings 17:3-4), so that God could take care of him there. In the safety and isolation of the wilderness, he could drink of the brook's water and be cared for by the birds that God sent to him.

This is an important lesson right from the beginning. Before Elijah performed any miracle or confronted any more power or made any more official pronouncements, he needed to experience the wilderness. He needed to learn what it would mean to be utterly dependent on God to provide all he needed.

The Bible is full of wilderness experiences. It is one of the most common set pieces on the entire biblical stage.

The Israelites were there, wandering for decades in a vast wilderness before they entered the Promised Land.

David was there, before he became king, fearing for his life from an enraged Saul.

John the Baptist was there. He turned the wilderness into his office, and the desert into his pulpit.

Even Jesus was there. Before he performed any miracles or uttered any teachings, he was there to experience the gravity of the human condition, and he discovered that it is one of suffering, temptation, and isolation.

If you are in the wilderness today, you are surrounded by a company of witnesses who are among the greatest of biblical heroes. And if even the greats of our faith suffered in the wilderness, don't feel so surprised that you do, too.

You might identify your wilderness as a physical hardship or mental anguish. You might be suffering the sting of shame and guilt from your past, or be fraught with anxiety about your future. Your wilderness might be littered with scorched relationships with people you have a hard time forgiving. Your wilderness might be a financial condition that is crumbling, or a job search that is going nowhere.

Your wilderness might be one of identity and acceptance as you struggle to find out who you really are and what you are meant to become. Or worse, you know who you are and are fearful that others might not accept you. And the cumulative result of all these things is that you are wondering where God is in the wilderness.

But notice something about each of the wilderness experiences in the Bible. In each case, people discovered that God was right there with them, in a way they would not have realized if they had not gone through that wilderness.

The Israelites were fed manna every day; just enough, no more and no less, to make it one day at a time. They had a pillar of fire lead them by night and a cloud by day, to remind them that God was always at hand.

David was blessed with strength and courage by God, and support from his beloved friend Jonathan and many others, to rise above his fears.

John the Baptist was blessed by his mission from God, with great anticipation for the One for whom he was preparing the way.

Jesus was nourished by the angels and his command of the Scriptures to withstand his trials by the devil.

And Elijah received bread from ravens and water from a brook to sustain him during his lonely time in the wilderness. Elijah learned the lesson those before him discovered and after him would also discover in the wilderness: depend on God, who is and will be with you.

This message is clear: if you are going to do the work of God in the world, you need to learn that your strength and your means will not be sufficient to get you through it. And sometimes, when you are in the wilderness time of your life, in pain, hardship, suffering, or anxiety, that may be *exactly* where God wants you to be in order to learn how to trust and depend on God. You can't learn that unless you are in the wilderness.

The Woman Who Hit Rock Bottom
1 Kings 17:8-24

Well, the respite at Cherith did not last long, as is often the case with moments of peace or preparation. Just like that, God gave Elijah his first major marching orders. He told him to travel to Zarephath, near Sidon in Phoenician territory, where he would meet a widow who would take care of him.

FINDING HOPE
IN HARD TIMES

What evidence do you see that God is giving you just enough strength and resources to make it one day at a time?

If you don't see such evidence now, what might you begin doing to strengthen your trust in God?

Elijah would soon discover that the nourishment and strength he gained from the ravens would be tested, as it was about an eighty-mile journey to that town. Of more concern the fact that he was heading into enemy territory. Sidon had a long history of oppressing the Israelite people, since back in the days of the Judges. Zarephath, where Elijah was heading, was on the Mediterranean coast in the same region. The area was associated with Phoenician rule and the worship of Baal.

Most importantly, Sidon was where Queen Jezebel herself had come from.

But this mission would be unlike many of Elijah's other ones. God would not be calling him into any royal palace. There would be no stern confrontation with someone in the seat of power, no declaration of rebuke. This time, the encounter would be distinctly personal, an intimate exchange with someone on the absolute opposite end of the power hierarchy. Elijah would be meeting a widow, who in that culture had no notable social status or means of self-sufficiency, someone who would have otherwise been ignored by the public, or at best would have struggled to make a living far from the centers of the world's power.

Except God noticed her.

When Elijah arrived at the town gate, likely famished from an arduous journey, he saw the woman, preparing for what she said would be the final meal for her and her son. Over the last few days, she had watched her flour and oil reserves shrink, and she had marked on her mental calendar the day when they would be down to that last meal. And today was that day.

I suspect many of us could identify with that woman. When we watch our bills rise and our incomes drop, we think about how long we have left in such an unsustainable condition. When the doctors give us or our loved ones the diagnosis we were dreading, we start thinking for the first time about a future filled with finish lines. When we first recognize that we may have more years behind us than ahead of us, we tremble at the thought of our own finiteness, where time is no longer our friend but an unrelenting force.

The widow explained all this to Elijah, in not so many words. "We'll eat the last of the food and then die" (1 Kings 17:12). Quite a lot to admit to a total stranger. But everything she said was in response to what we would think to be quite a brash request. Elijah asked her to make him a meal.

It's true that Elijah was simply acting on the promise that God had given him, that this widow would care for his needs. But as much as we might admire his courage in the upcoming stories, like speaking truth to the powerful Ahab and Jezebel, staring down the prophets of Baal on the mountain, or any other act of power he would perform, what he asked of this woman took sheer guts. (*I can see you're impoverished, ma'am. And I know you are a widow with no real means to support yourself. But I'm hungry. And not only am I asking you to make me some food, I'm asking you to feed me first, and your son second. Okay?*)

Whew. Elijah had more guts than I would have had.

What is interesting about this encounter is just how needy both Elijah and the widow were. Elijah was suffering from physical hunger, and he had a strong desire to follow God's commands on his life. The widow was suffering from emotional, social, and financial distress, living with a reality for which she saw no positive outcome. It was an intersection of anguish, a meeting of two desperate souls looking to each other for help.

And that's just the way God often wants it.

During my first year in seminary, I worked in a local emergency overnight homeless shelter in downtown Dayton, Ohio. Every night, men, women, and children would come in off the streets seeking a warm bed, a hot meal, and a hot shower to make it through the night, so they could go out and face the next day. The director sat me down one day and told me his observations of what went on every night at the shelter.

"Magrey," he said, "every night two groups of people come in through the doors of the shelter. The first group comes in through the front door. They are the hungry, the homeless, the people who are left with virtually nothing except the will to survive. They come seeking food, a bed, and a chance. They have real needs.

"The second group," he said, "comes in through the back door. They are the volunteers who come in with a meal to serve our guests. They will give of their time and their means to serve a hot plate of food with a warm smile and an openness to treat these men and women as human beings. They have needs, too. A need to feel like they are making a difference in the world. A need to feel like they are using their talents and their time for God's kingdom. A need to fulfill their purpose in life.

"Magrey, when all those people come in, the group through the front door and the group through the back door, when those two different sets of needs meet in the center of the shelter, around the dining tables, and share a meal together—that is when the church happens."

I've never forgotten his definition of church, one of the best I've ever heard. Church happens when people's needs are met by those who need to serve.

Back in Zarephath, right there on the front edge of an ancient coastal village, when a weary traveler encountered a desperate widow, a community of faith was formed. Elijah had his needs: the need to follow God's call on his life, the need to have his hunger met and his energy restored. The widow had her needs as well: the need for food for her and her young son, the need for hope amid her hard times. And both of them had this: the need to have their faith in God renewed, with some reminder that God was by their side.

It was in that moment, when their needs met in the holy intersection of divine ethos and human pathos, that God's grace became vividly real to them. The oil and flour did not run out; God provided day after day.

How about you? Are you part of a church community where you are both a container and a conduit of God's grace? One in which you recognize the privilege and responsibility of receiving and giving glimpses of God's love and generosity with others? Whatever needs you might have, God has drawn someone within that community of faith to meet you in precisely the right way. And even if you feel like you have very little to give, like you are down to your last bits of flour and drops of oil, you still have something to offer.

That's just the way God works. When we feel like we have hit rock bottom, there appears a foothold. When we feel like we are sinking, a buoy bobs on the horizon. When we feel like we are in a free fall, we feel a rip cord to pull. Sometimes, these moments don't guarantee an immediate turnaround, but they are enough.

This is the way God often works. To give you just enough to get you through the day, nothing more and nothing less.

Again, just like in the last story, it is hard to hear this tale without noticing the echoes from the Israelites in Exodus. When they were wandering nomads in the wilderness, God gave the Israelites bread to eat in the form of manna. It came as a mere one-day supply, to be replenished one day at a time.

We might also think about Jesus' feeding of the multitude, the only miracle other than the Resurrection to be recorded in all four Gospels. Just when there appeared to be no means to feed the masses of hungry people, Jesus found a way and even had leftovers.

When you think about it that way, then Elijah, Moses, and Jesus all experienced firsthand God's ability to provide for God's people when all seemed hopeless and lost. So it ought to be no wonder that these three would enjoy a remarkable reunion on the Mount of Transfiguration in the Gospels. They represented the goodness, power, and provision of a generous God who loves to give us "our daily bread."

When Grief Strikes Suddenly

It would be great if the story of Elijah and the widow ended here, with full stomachs, buoyed hopes, and an invigorated deter-mination by the widow to ride out the drought until it ended. But just like life, there was a curveball right around the corner.

The widow's son, her greatest treasure on earth, suddenly became ill and died. Just when you thought life could not get any tougher for this woman, the bottom completely fell out from under her. Her downward spiral of grief was marked with anguished cries like those of many we know who have grieved, perhaps including yourself.

Why has this happened to me?

Did God cause this to happen?

Is this God's way of punishing me?

The woman wondered all these questions, and then she went one step further: "What's gone wrong between us, man of God?" she asked Elijah. "Have you come to me to call attention to my sin and kill my son?" (1 Kings 17:18).

This may have been her anger talking, but we don't blame her. When grief strikes like a thief in the night, we are often left with little rationality to sustain us. We begin drifting into the dark places of our spirits, uncharted territories that are not illuminated by clarity, conviction, and love. We might call it "a dark night of the soul," like the one St. John of the Cross wrote about. Or a "contradiction in the soul," as Mother Teresa described it. You might have your own description of it in your own spiritual autobiography.

In the first Zarephath story, the woman was worried about her provisions running dry. Now, she was worried about her convictions running out. Her whole way of looking at the world, as well as her ability to trust God and this messenger of God, was now called into question.

And it was a good thing that Elijah carried the boy up to the bedroom, out of earshot of the woman. Because if he hadn't, she would have heard Elijah pretty much wrestling with God over the same questions. "LORD my God, why is it that you have brought such evil upon the widow that I am staying with by killing her son?" he cried (1 Kings 17:20).

If the fact that Elijah and this widow dared to accuse God of doing this to her son surprises you, then look at it this way: God could handle their questions, embrace their doubts, and even allow their skepticism and anger. And God can handle yours. Look at the

Psalms, or Job, or Lamentations. Look at Jacob wrestling with the angel, Paul wrestling with the thorn in his flesh, and even Jesus himself wrestling with his mission in the garden of Gethsemane.

If there is anything we learn about Elijah and this widow, it is that even though they were mystified and even upset about God's role in their suffering, they did not question God's ability to hear them amid their suffering. They might have questioned God's timing or methodology. But they did not question God's presence or attentiveness to their cries.

Perhaps that is an encouraging word that you need to hear. God is with you, even if you are struggling with who God is or why God does what God does.

In the end, God raised the boy back to life. Whatever happened as Elijah lay across the boy three times and cried out, "Lord my God, please give this boy's life back to him" (1 Kings 17:21), it was enough to resurrect him from the dead. But by then, another miracle had already occurred. It was found in two people—Elijah and the widow—whose belief in God's attentiveness to their needs remained unshaken. It was found in their willingness to bare their souls raw, before a God who knew the condition of their souls to begin with. And it was found in a God who not only received their cries, but transformed them into possibilities of hope and new life.

The miracle is found in a God who can do the same for you.

Outnumbered, but Not Overpowered
1 Kings 18:1-40

It was now three years into the great drought, and you can imagine the toll it had to be taking on the people. Food and water

FINDING HOPE
IN HARD TIMES

In what ways do you feel down to your "last bit of oil and flour"?

Do you know someone else who might be experiencing something similar?

How might God be calling you to be both a container and a conduit of God's grace and love?

were scarce, anxieties high, and hopes low. And at the center of it all was Elijah, the man whose pronouncement ushered in the calamity from the start.

Ahab was fuming. He was not going to be bested by some commoner, he would not let his rule be tarnished by bad weather, and there was no way the God of Elijah was going to outdo the god of his wife Jezebel. Ahab started looking for Elijah everywhere. And we know what would have happened if Ahab had found him—Jezebel had already killed most of the Lord's prophets, after all (1 Kings 18:4).

Elijah had a death sentence over his head.

If this reaction sounds familiar, it ought to. One of the recurring motifs throughout the Bible is the ongoing conflict between the kingdom of God and the kingdoms of this world. Think about Moses vs. Pharaoh, David vs. Goliath, Daniel vs. Nebuchadnezzar, or even Jesus vs. Pilate. Time and again, we see an ongoing refrain of the battle between the "love of power" and "powerless love," between the ways of the world, which hoard power and protect it with paranoia and violence, and the ways of God, which call for self-sacrifice, fidelity, and love.

At the outset of 1 Kings 18, this has all the makings of a heavyweight title bout.

But before we get to the main event, we get an intriguing undercard.

Caught Between Loyalties

We meet a man named Obadiah and quickly learn two things about him. He was a high-ranking official in the palace of Ahab and Jezebel, a kind of royal chief of staff, employed to carry out whatever orders they demanded and keep everything in order. He was also a man who feared God, called to follow God's righteous and holy ways. He lived daily at a crossroads between his secular responsibilities and his religious convictions, which had to make his life terribly difficult.

You might be able to identify with his dilemma. If you've ever had to work for a company whose business practices took short-cuts with ethics and morals, you have felt his crisis of conflicted convictions.

If you've ever had to make the hard choice between maintaining your family's dysfunctional status quo or taking the more difficult road of intervention and health, you know the hard choice he had to make.

If you've ever been tempted to take the quick and easy route toward achievement and success instead of doing the right thing, which might cost you everything you've worked for, you know what it was like to be Obadiah.

He maintained the uneasy balance every day. He stood with one foot on the dock of political power and influence, and his other foot on the boat of his commitment to God—all while the increasing currents of life's complexity kept pulling the two apart.

Eventually, he began moonlighting as a protector of God's prophets, hiding a hundred of them away in a cave when Jezebel began killing them. He gave them precious provisions of food and water to keep them alive, despite the drought that made such provisions hard to come by. Every day, he put his reputation and his life on the line, living a double life that made him fearful.

It is not easy to be torn between loyalties.

But he had earned Ahab's trust. When Ahab went looking for water during the severe drought in Israel, he took Obadiah along and instructed him to go off in a different direction to cover the terrain more effectively.

And that's when Obadiah bumped into Elijah.

You can imagine the mixed emotions that had to course through Obadiah's conscience. Here was Elijah, the great man of faith, the foremost messenger of God in the land. But he was also the very man whom his master Ahab would have loved to see dead. And when his conflicted emotions settled, and Elijah told Obadiah to tell Ahab that he was ready to meet him, Obadiah realized the one who was in real trouble in this moment was not Elijah, but Obadiah himself.

Obadiah was skeptical. A man like Elijah, who had been on the run and in hiding for the last three years, surely wasn't going to just turn himself over, was he? Obadiah thought he knew exactly what Elijah must have been up to: As Obadiah was going to tell Ahab that he found Elijah, Elijah was surely going to run away again. And when Ahab showed up and found Obadiah was lying, he was going to kill his chief of staff.

After all these years of living a double life, succeeding in his profession while maintaining his faith convictions, everything was about to fall apart. It was a watershed moment for a man who had a very difficult choice to make.

In the end, Obadiah chose to honor his fidelity to God over his commitment to his boss. He brought Elijah's message to Ahab, at risk to his own life, trusting Elijah's promise in God's name that he would indeed meet with the king of Israel. Obadiah chose to serve the one who gave him life, rather than the one who used him for death. It was not an easy choice, but it was the right one. And you can make the same right choice, too.

The Showdown

When Elijah and Ahab finally met face to face, Elijah offered a unique way of settling the conflict and deciding who was right once and for all. They wouldn't duke it out or debate, but they would have a contest. A contest involving two altars.

Elijah said, "Okay, Ahab. Let's settle this now. Take all your prophets, all the ones that help you worship the foreign god Baal. And combine them with the 400 prophets that serve your wife's god, Asherah. That's 850 prophets. And let's have them go up against the prophets of God, Yahweh. Now, as you know you've pretty much killed all the prophets of Yahweh except me, so that basically leaves it as a battle between 850 and 1. How does that sound? A showdown on top of Mount Carmel today."

Ahab, naturally, was no fool. He knew a sure thing when he saw it. More than eight hundred of his own versus one man of God. No problem. He liked those odds. So he agreed to Elijah's terms.

Elijah explained the rules. Instead of hand-to-hand combat and a fight to the death, this would be a fight to the fire. The first team to have their god (God) send fire down from heaven was going to win.

So, if you can imagine, the playing field was simple. Two altars. One for the 850, one for Elijah. One for Baal, the other for Yahweh. One for the false god, and one for the only true God.

And here is where things get really interesting for you and me. Because it is at this point that we start to get this eerie feeling that we have heard this story before. We have felt this story before. We have lived this story before.

You see, it is quite possible that what makes this story so important for us to hear is not that it is a story of us versus them. This is not about Christians taking on the world. It is not about us holy-roller, high-and-mighties trying to defeat the forces of evil in the world today.

Both altars, in fact, reside within each of our own souls. Each of us has an altar to God in our lives, an impulse and a longing to worship the true God. Yet each of us also has an altar erected within our hearts to worship the false idols of our lives. We may not realize it, but we do.

For some of us, that altar is built to the false god of achievement, social status, or wealth. We feel like if we can accumulate, climb the ladder, or at least look better than everyone else, then we are making it.

For some of us, that altar is built on a top-heavy reliance on human institutions to provide a kind of salvation that only God can provide. We turn to political campaigns, military might, and economic engines to ensure that we are going to be okay, based on the belief that God is on our side.

That's what is really at the heart of this story. It is the question of what kind of God we really believe in. Do we believe in a god who is only here to be a giant vending machine or a cosmic butler to serve our needs on our terms, to do what we ask, when we ask for it?

If that's the case, then we really are a lot like the 850 prophets of Baal.

They went first. They gathered the driest wood they could find. They slaughtered the animal for sacrifice and placed it on the top.

They prayed to Baal. Then they waited. And waited. And they prayed some more. But nothing. Hours passed, and there was no fire.

Elijah was enjoying this. He jumped in and said to the prophets, "You know, uh, maybe your god's asleep. Maybe you should, you know, get louder." So they did. They yelled. And they started dancing and flailing. Desperate to get the god's attention, they took out their knives and starting cutting up their bodies and letting the blood pour out. But they couldn't get that fire started.

You see, this is what happens when we are worshiping a false god. We'll spend lots of time searching for the right change and banging on the vending machine without getting what we want. We'll spend lots of energy demanding and ordering the butler to obey us, not realizing that God is not a butler at all.

By the time we see the 850 give up and Elijah step up, we almost know already how the story is going to end. We know that God is going to rain down the fire, and that God is going to deliver. Yes, Elijah rubs it in first by dousing the altar with five jugs of water, drenching it, filling the moat, soaking the animal, turning the altar into a mud pit. But we still know how it's going to end.

God sends fire to consume the altar. By the time we see what God has done, turning every single drop of moisture to steam and the mud to char, and we watch the 850 standing there in disbelief, we shouldn't be surprised.

Until we realize this: we're standing next to the other altar.

Oh, there is plenty of conflict in this story. But to say that we are Elijah and that Baal is found in other people and throughout our culture would make it much too easy to let ourselves off the hook. If we really do think about it and take a serious inventory of our spiritual lives, we will discover not just one, but multiple altars, built to many false gods that we turn to for the kind of security that only God can provide.

And if it has been a while since you've witnessed God's victorious fire raining down on your life, maybe it's because you've been standing next to the wrong altar.

Maybe, as you think about this story and your place in it, and as the Spirit opens up your heart and mind to the condition of your soul, you might choose to step toward the altar of God and step away from the other altars in yourself that you have built for the false gods in your life.

Then perhaps you can affirm for yourself what all the people eventually realized in 1 Kings 18:39: "The LORD is the real God!

FINDING HOPE
IN HARD TIMES

What are the false gods in your life to whom you have erected altars in your soul?

What can you do to step away from the wrong altar and align yourself with the altar of God?

CHAPTER 2
WHEN YOU FEEL DOWN AND OUT

CHAPTER 2

WHEN YOU FEEL DOWN AND OUT

Wouldn't it be great if hope always rained down in ways that are bold and obvious, like the fire that poured down on the altar of Mount Carmel? It would make the hardships of life so much easier to bear, knowing that the next respite is as clearly marked as an interstate rest area sign.

But that's not always the case when you feel down and out. Sometimes, hope comes in the small and subtle. In ways that seem so imperceptible that you really have to watch for it, and really have to listen for it.

Elijah was about to learn that lesson. And so should we.

Hope the Size of a Small Cloud
1 Kings 18:41-46

God wasn't finished.

In 1 Kings 18, there is barely a narrative breath between verses 40 and 41, between the end of the fiery face-off on Mount Carmel and the next big story. We would expect that Elijah would have at least been afforded a breather, a chance to sit back and marvel at the victory he had just witnessed. It's not every day that you see such a definitive demonstration of God's power, in such a clear and convincing victory. But he didn't even have a chance to kick up his feet for a minute before God pushed him to the next stage of his mission. He told Ahab to prepare for the long-awaited end of the drought with the oddest of instructions: eat and drink. Throw a party. Celebrate. The rain is coming.

The story does not have to go any further before we already sense what an unusual tale this is going to be. Elijah was so sure of his divinely drawn convictions that he felt no need to hedge his bets when it came to Ahab. If it were you or I, we might say, "Um, Ahab, rain may be coming." Or, "There's a chance something is going to happen." Or, "You might want to pull out that dusty raincoat, check your roof for leaks, and gather up your umbrellas." But Elijah boldly said, "Celebrate with food and drink because I hear the sound of a rainstorm coming" (1 Kings 18:41).

The way Elijah chose to mark God's victory on Mount Carmel was not to relax and relish or to step back and savor, but to ride the momentum of God's victory into the next challenge. This is a man who had clearly found his element in God's work, and he was ready to move on it.

The spiritual principle at work here is that in every given moment, God is always at work, drawing us forward into the next movement of grace. When times seem tough and our situation seems at its lowest, God is already a step ahead, buoying us up and prompting us forward. And even when things seem to be going well, God is preparing us for the next step into the ever-changing, ever-challenging adventure of spiritual maturity.

Think about the life of Jesus. He experienced the remarkable gift of baptism by John in the Jordan, then was *immediately* driven by the Spirit into the wilderness to be tempted. He was on the mountaintop of Transfiguration, hearing how pleased the Father was with him, then *immediately* told the disciples they could not stay there—they all went down the mountain to minister to the needs of the masses below. Jesus experienced the glory of God's provision in the feeding of a hungry multitude, then soon had to save the disciples from sure shipwreck in a storm.

This is not to say that we should not have times of rest, reflection, and renewal. Those times are critical, and they are clearly replete throughout Elijah's life. We need moments like the ravens feeding him at the Cherith, or the encounter in Mount Horeb (in the next chapter) to breathe and remember.

But God is always at work. God is always anticipating our next steps. God is never finished.

And thank goodness that's the case. Paul said to the church in Philippi, "I'm sure about this: the one who started a good work in you will stay with you to complete the job by the day of Christ Jesus" (Philippians 1:6). The psalmist described God's constant work in our lives and in the world in Psalm 121, with the assurance that God never takes a break:

I raise my eyes toward the mountains.
    Where will my help come from?
My help comes from the LORD,
    the maker of heaven and earth.
God won't let your foot slip.
    Your protector won't fall asleep on the job.
No! Israel's protector
    never sleeps or rests!

(Psalm 121:1-4)

God is tenacious and tireless, and is in relentless pursuit of the long-term goal: the full restoration of the whole created order back to the way God intended it. The kingdom on earth, as it is in heaven.

What happened next in the life of Elijah was an opportunity for him to demonstrate his own tenacity and patience. He went back up to the top of Mount Carmel, the scene of his most recent victory, and bent over onto the ground in a position of prayer and receptivity. He then turned to his servant and told him to check the skies for the latest weather report. Time to look for evidence that the forecast the Divine Meteorologist had given him was coming true.

Nope, the servant reported. Not a cloud in sight. Blue skies, sunny day, and a perfect day for a picnic—but not for an outdoor shower.

We aren't told exactly what Elijah was thinking in that moment. The generous reader among us would want to believe that Elijah was unfazed the first, second, third, and fourth times that the servant came back with the same report from the skies. But you and I know very well what we would have been feeling. We would have felt skepticism and suspicion. Irritation and anger.

Especially when we had just learned that God is never finished, always working, constantly moving forward, we would think that there would surely be evidence to support those claims on demand, whenever we need it to cure our own inbred incredulity.

Think about the number of times in the Bible someone had to exercise remarkable patience in order to follow God. Jacob labored for seven years to earn the right to marry Rachel, only to be deceived by her father Laban into working for seven more. The Israelites left Egypt and journeyed to the Promised Land, only to be sentenced to forty years of wilderness wandering because of their disobedience. Naaman, as we will see in the story of Elisha, had to dip himself into the Jordan River seven times in order to be healed of his leprosy. A blind man in the Gospels had to have Jesus touch his eyes a second time in order to have his eyesight fully cleared.

Oftentimes in the Bible, miracles happen instantaneously. So it's easy to lose heart when God's promises aren't fulfilled on our timeline, under our expectations. It gets even more frustrating when we find ourselves on a roller coaster of anticipation, followed by disappointment, followed by hope, followed by hopelessness, only to see the cycle repeat itself. This is what happened to Elijah, and it had to have happened to his servant as well.

And think about his servant, after the fifth or sixth time of getting up, hoofing it out to the edge of the mountain, squinting over the water, craning his neck up to the sky, only to see the same thing he had seen every disappointing time before.

It's not hard to imagine what he was thinking. We've been there. So have loved ones.

The latest round of scans reveals no shrinkage in the tumor, even though you were sure this round of chemo made a difference.

Another month has come and gone, and you and your spouse still haven't conceived a child.

Yet another overture to repair the breach of a broken relationship with a friend has not been returned in kind, so you both are still in a state of limbo.

Another night has gone by, and that nagging temptation or addiction is no more tamed than it was when the beast first assaulted your senses years ago.

I think it's important that this story immediately follows the episode on Mount Carmel. Back on the mountaintop, success was quick, indisputable, and complete. Elijah prayed, God responded, and there was no hesitation in God's demonstration of power. It literally was a mountaintop experience, much like the ones that dot the happy landscapes of our spiritual lives.

But just as quickly as the Mount Carmel story ends, a contrasting story begins. This one reminds us that even though God never stops working and God is always faithful, God's timing is rarely predictable. After all, if it were, then God would be acting on our terms, based on our expectations.

And there would be no need for faith.

That's always the kicker, isn't it? Faith is like a double-edged tool. It helps us through the tough times, but it requires that we go through the tough times. It reminds us that we are not God, but it alleviates the pressure of being like God. It calls us to step outside our comfort zone, but reminds us that that is always the best place to be.

By the time Elijah and his servant got to the sixth go-around of staring-studying-sulking-returning, it must have taken all kinds of inner resources for Elijah to turn to his servant again and say, "You know what to do. Do it again."

It would make you wonder what the servant was thinking. It might have been, "Okay, Elijah. But you know what I'm going to say." Or, "Why don't you check it out for yourself? I'm tired." Or, "Fine. But I'm not getting my hopes up."

But maybe, just maybe, there was a little voice that was speaking to both of them that time. Maybe there was a small voice that said, "Remember, all it takes is once. All God needs is one shot. It doesn't matter if it comes the first time, the seventh time, or the seventieth time. Just one."

And sure enough, the seventh time worked.

It's interesting. If you read a bit between the lines of verse 44, the servant wasn't exactly sold on the report. It would have been a lot more compelling—and a lot more convincing—if the servant had seen a huge storm front rolling in from the horizon. The kind of dark, foreboding, exhilarating, inspiring storms you sometimes see when you can *feel* it coming toward you.

But that's not what he saw. He saw a single cloud. If you can even call it a cloud. More like a wisp, a tuft, a speck of white, as small as a human hand on the horizon.

And that's all that God needs.

Often, God doesn't work through massive storm fronts, with lightning bolts and thunderclaps that leave no doubt of where you stand or where you are going. The biblical record is filled with reminders that God much prefers to speak through burning bushes, mustard seeds, or an innocent baby gift-wrapped in swaddling clothes. The need, the expectation for God to work in the realms of the majestic and unmistakable may be *our* need, but it's not always God's preference.

Still, that's all God needed. The rains came, with dark clouds and a huge storm all from that tiny cloud as a beginning. A hand-sized cloud in the hands of the Creator is enough to turn around even the most dire situation. It is a recurring theme throughout the stories of Elijah and Elisha. A pile of wet wood surrounded by a moat, a drop or two of oil, a still small voice: these may seem insignificant and even impossible against the odds. But in God's hands, they're enough. They're more than enough.

If anything, this story reminds us that God doesn't always work according to our time line or our method. Faith calls us to stretch beyond what we think we need, and the timing in which we think we need it, and trust that God is always working. God never rests. God is always moving.

And God is giving you the strength to keep on trusting, keep on going, keep on looking. One more time, and maybe even seven.

Elijah and the Still Small Voice
1 Kings 19:1-18

Let's just say that when Jezebel found out about what Elijah had done to the prophets of Baal, she was not pleased. Jezebel was now left with a crippled arsenal of prophets and, more importantly, a deeply bruised ego. And as Elijah well knew, an angry Jezebel was a dangerous and wicked Jezebel.

Jezebel put a death warrant out on Elijah's head, sending him a message that she vowed to kill him "by this time tomorrow" (1 Kings 19:2). Then Elijah did what any sensible, rational, clear-thinking person like you and me would have done. He ran screaming for his life out into the wilderness. After a day of running, he collapsed, exhausted, under a broom bush. Elijah cried out to God with words that are as painful as they are poignant, as raw as they are real: "It's more than enough, LORD! Take my life because I'm no better than my ancestors" (1 Kings 19:4).

FINDING HOPE
IN HARD TIMES

When has God ever worked in your life in a way that was contrary to the timing and method you expected from God?

How might God be calling you to exercise your faith to hang in there, despite the lack of evidence of God's activity in your life?

What might that "small cloud" look like to you?

Certainly, of the many things that we learn about Elijah in the Bible, I think this is the phrase that makes him the most human, the most approachable, and the most relevant to us. Odds are you have experienced this level of frustration and fatigue before in your life.

When have you ever been completely and totally worn down by the pressures of life and the demands of daily living?

As you tried to negotiate an unceasing barrage of daily responsibilities?

As you discovered that you are trying to wear too many hats at once, and they don't all fit on your head?

As you dealt with doubt in your life, and struggled to reconcile your reason with the unfathomable mysteries of the faith?

Or maybe you are in the middle of a kind of dry spell, where you are yearning for something more in your life, a sense of passion, thrill, or excitement that can captivate your imagination and energy.

If any of this describes you, then you've got a patron saint here in the person of Elijah.

In the Disney/Pixar movie *The Incredibles*, the main hero, Bob Parr, is a former super hero who fled into hiding after it became illegal for super heroes to use their powers in public. A disheartened, bored, and exhausted Bob Parr, a.k.a. Mr. Incredible, comes home from a tedious day in the office only to find a neighborhood boy in his driveway. The boy looks up at Bob and stares at him, having seen evidence of his super-hero potential earlier. Bob finally asks the boy, "What are you waiting for?" To which the boy says, "I don't know . . . something amazing, I guess!" Bob sighs. "Me too, kid," he says.

That's the line, isn't it? For anyone and everyone who is wandering in the wilderness, that's what we are waiting for. We're looking for something surprising and exciting to intervene in our lives and give us a new spark of energy and zeal to punctuate our realities.

And that is exactly the message that came to Elijah.

Well, sort of.

What we are about to learn is that God does show up, just not always the way we expect.

After an angel nourished Elijah with a little food and water, the angel said to him, "Get up! . . . Eat something, because you have a difficult road ahead of you" (1 Kings 19:7). Elijah ate and drank, then journeyed for forty days and nights to the mountain of God, Mount Horeb.

Mount Horeb is another name for Mount Sinai, the mountain where God appeared to Moses in a burning bush and later gave the Ten Commandments to the Israelites. This is the mountain associated with God's presence and power. Elijah went there, by a long and difficult road, hoping to hear from God.

Elijah must have thought to himself that something exciting was bound to happen there. Something amazing. The mountain was the place we would expect God to show up. This particular mountain is where God met Moses and the Israelites. A mountain is where Jesus gave his best sermon, prayed for his life, and ultimately died on a cross. Of all the places that we would expect Elijah to find God, it would have to be on a mountain, wouldn't it?

What's significant, though, is that Elijah went into a cave on the mountain. A cave is not a place to find God in spectacular vistas, but a place to experience mystery. Caves are places of resignation, not revelation. They are places you go if you want to experience containment, concealment, and death. They are mythological places of the underworld, leading into the deepest, most impenetrable places of the unconscious. Think about David, hiding for his life in a cave out of fear of King Saul. Or the kind of cave that Jonah lived in for three nights, the belly of a fish. And think of the cave where Jesus was buried after his death. Caves are places of darkness.

And think about the way that your life may be in a cave right now. Concealed, confined, dark, lonely, isolated. Longing for light, yearning for freedom. This is where Elijah found himself when God spoke to him: "Why are you here, Elijah?" (1 Kings 19:9).

Maybe a cave can also be like a womb: a place where one must reside in order to emerge with new life. A place of rebirth. A place one must enter if one is to come out transformed and made new. In the cave is where God first showed up to Elijah. Elijah told God,

> *"I've been very passionate for the LORD God*
> *of heavenly forces because the Israelites have*
> *abandoned your covenant. They have torn down*
> *your altars, and they have murdered your prophets*
> *with the sword. I'm the only one left, and now they*
> *want to take my life too!"*
>
> (1 Kings 19:10)

In response, God promised to appear before Elijah. "Go out and stand at the mountain before the LORD. The LORD is passing by" (verse 11).

If you heard a voice from God saying that God was going to visit you and make an unmistakable appearance, you would be jolted to your feet with excitement. That had to be what was going through Elijah's mind. "Oh boy, oh boy, oh boy, oh boy, finally an end to this misery and this despair! God is coming."

Well, sort of.

The first thing that came by was a great wind. We would expect to find God in the wind. After all, this is the kind of wind that first hovered over the face of the waters, when the Spirit of God was present at Creation. It was like the wind that was breathed into human beings the moment human life began. It was like the wind and cloud present in the Tabernacle when it settled in among the wandering Israelites, or the wind that was heard when the Spirit touched down at Pentecost. If ever there was going to be a way for God to be made known to Elijah, surely it was through the wind.

But God was not in the wind. Because God is not always found in the way you've found God before.

Then came the earthquake. Yes, indeed, surely God would be in the earthquake. The same God who created the planets and fashioned the trees, rocks, and animals could shake the earth at its foundations. We remember that an earthquake accompanied the tearing of the Temple curtain at the time of Jesus' death, and an earthquake shook apart a jail cell where Paul and Silas were imprisoned. Surely, if ever there was a way for God to be made known to Elijah, it was here, in an earthquake.

But God was not in the earthquake. Because God is not always found in the way you've found God before.

Then came the fire. Certainly, God had to be in the fire. Like the fire that led the Israelites through the wilderness by night, a pillar of fire that blazed the way. Or the fire that touched down like tongues at Pentecost. Well, even Elijah himself had just witnessed the fire of God through the servant showdown on Mount Carmel. If ever there was a way we would expect God to be revealed to Elijah, it had to be through the fire.

But God was not in the fire. Because God is not always found in the way we have found God before.

What does all of this teach us? That sometimes, when we look for God in the ways we have found God in the past, we are unable to find God. Sometimes we don't find God in the wind, the earthquake, or the fire. Maybe not even on top of the mountain at all. We don't always discover God in the standard prayers that we have prayed or in the small group of Scriptures we have read over and over again. Nor do we find God always in the places, behaviors, or times that we have met God in the past. What this reminds us of is that we cannot view God as a genie in a bottle, there to be summoned if we rub the right way or utter the right incantations. We cannot treat God as a lucky rabbit's foot, there at our disposal whenever we need it. No, if that were the case, then we would be god over God.

Instead, what this passage teaches us is that we need to leave room in our hearts and our minds for God to surprise us, to break out of our preconceived notions and the boxes where we have placed God. Sometimes what's needed is simply for us to quiet our thoughts and our minds and listen and watch for God to work.

It was not until Elijah had dispelled all of those closely held assumptions about God that God was able, finally, to break through to him. The Bible says that eventually, Elijah heard "a sound. Thin. Quiet" (1 Kings 19:12). Other translations call it "a sound of sheer silence" (NRSV) or "a still small voice" (KJV).

A voice, thin and quiet, came to Elijah. A whisper, just a bit louder than the noise within his heart, that finally said to him, "What are you doing here, Elijah?" (1 Kings 19:13 NRSV).

And Elijah told God again how lonely he was, how tired and fearful he was. Now, when Elijah was finally able to be quiet and

FINDING HOPE
IN HARD TIMES

How hard is it for you to quiet all the noise in your life and create space for silence?

How might you let go of your preconceived means of experiencing God and be open to some new way for God to be revealed to you?

What might that still small voice be saying to you right now?

listen, God spoke words of encouragement to him, and God showed him the next step in his journey.

The key to experiencing something new, surprising, and amazing—the key to overcoming spiritual dryness and total exhaustion—is to quiet your life down and listen.

Perhaps the best thing you can do right now is to sit in silence and soak in the presence of God. You might choose to close this book for a few moments and practice some centering prayer. Get yourself in a seated position in a comfortable chair, with your feet flat on the floor, your back straight, and your hands palms down or palms up on your lap, in a receptive position.

Choose a centering word to repeat in your mind when you feel your thoughts starting to wander, like *Abba*, *Maranatha*, *peace*, or *shalom*. Close your eyes and take a few deep breaths to quiet yourself. For a period of time, five minutes, or ten, or fifteen or more, sit in the silence of God. Quiet your mind. Allow the presence of the Spirit to fill you, comfort you, encourage you, and give you the strength to go on.

☙ When Envy Consumes You
1 Kings 21:1-16

One thing we have come to understand in reading the Bible is that we can learn a lot about ourselves by studying the characters in it. On many occasions, we can learn from the virtues of biblical people: the faith of Abraham, the courage of Esther, the wisdom of Deborah, the passion of David. There are also many occasions when we should learn from the mistakes of its people. Aside from Jesus, every person in the Bible is depicted with both admirable and negative traits, so that we can learn from their positive examples as well as from their errors. That's one of the beauties of the Bible. It is unafraid to render people honestly, without sugar-coating them when they go bad.

That is especially true of the main characters in this reading. First, there is Ahab. He had two palaces. That's how rich he was. He had one palace in Samaria and a second palace in Jezreel, one of which the Bible tells us was made of ivory (1 Kings 22:39). So, imagine the largest house you can, the largest mansion you've ever seen, then picture that mansion covered, from floor to ceiling, with ivory carvings. Can you imagine? Ahab also had seventy sons, meaning Jezebel clearly wasn't his only wife.

The point is this: Ahab was pretty well off, and whatever he wanted, he could have gotten.

One day, he was in his palace, perhaps surrounded by these luxurious ivory carvings. He looked out the window and saw a patch of land that he knew he didn't own. It was a vineyard that belonged to a man named Naboth.

He thought, "That would be a great place for me to plant a garden. Right there outside my window. Perfect." So, he went to Naboth and said, "Give me your vineyard so it can become my vegetable garden, because it is right next to my palace. In exchange for it, I'll give you an even better vineyard. Or if you prefer, I'll pay you the price in silver" (1 Kings 21:2).

To which Naboth responded, No. "Lord forbid that I give you my family inheritance!" (verse 3). Naboth can't do it, and he seems even angered by the request. He seems to be saying, "I can't do that. It has belonged to my family for generations, it is our source of income. It isn't much, but it's been in my family forever."

I can imagine Ahab pressing the offer. "C'mon. I'll give you anything for it."

But Naboth held fast to his property and refused to sell. He reminded Ahab that even the law of God says we are not to sell our inheritance. No, Ahab. You can't have it.

So, Ahab slumped back to his palace and pouted. He was depressed. He was so down that he didn't eat. He could have purchased any other property, or forgotten about the vineyard and moved on to something else. But instead, he was fixated on the one little thing he couldn't have.

The question for you and me is, "Is there a bit of Ahab within each of us?" I suggest that there is, without a doubt. There's a piece of us that treats possessions as more important than people. Pride over compassion. Greed over equality and fairness.

I don't know what that object of covetousness would be for you. Maybe it literally is a piece of land. Or it could be some other kind of material possession, like a piece of jewelry, an article of clothing, a piece of equipment, or a luxury item. It may be something you don't need, but that's beside the point. Whatever it may be, it serves to cover up whatever insecurity, fill whatever hole, or feed whatever kind of need for achievement or pride you might have.

Whatever that is, we have a bit of Ahab within us.

Now what about Jezebel? As we know, she was just as bad as Ahab. Rather than trying to calm Ahab down and convince him that he didn't need that vineyard anyway and teaching him to be content, she decided to do something absolutely dastardly.

Jezebel wrote a letter to the elders of Jezreel, and told them, "Announce a fast and place Naboth at the head of the people. Then bring in two liars in front of him and have them testify as follows:

'You cursed God and king!' Then take Naboth outside and stone him so he dies" (1 Kings 21:9-10). Jezebel got people to testify that Naboth has cursed God and king—blasphemy and insurrection, punishable by death. The elders did what Jezebel said, and Naboth was stoned to death. Ahab was then able to go and take possession of Naboth's vineyard.

In response to this we have to ask ourselves, "What kind of person does this? What was she thinking?"

What we learn from Jezebel is that having power and authority over people does not give you license to treat them badly . . . but the temptation to do so can easily come with power. Ahab's problem was having too much wealth and treating others badly. Jezebel's problem was one of abusing her authority at the expense of others.

Lord Acton, the nineteenth-century British historian, offered this famous saying: "All power tends to corrupt; absolute power corrupts absolutely."

Jezebel's life exemplified that maxim, and her murder of Naboth illustrates it perfectly. The man was entirely innocent, but because she had the power and because her husband wanted what belonged to him, she had him killed on blatantly false charges.

Here's the lesson for each of us. When we are in a position of power and authority, we need to respect and love other people. Having influence does not give you an excuse to abuse someone else. We still need to treat other people with respect.

If you are in a restaurant and the server makes a mistake or treats you badly or screws something up, it does not give you an excuse to fly off the handle or refuse to leave a tip or do something vindictive.

If your children mess up, you as a parent still have to be the adult and treat your kids with kindness and respect, loving them with your actions and words. Discipline them, yes, but not to the point of belittling or abuse.

If you are in the workplace and you have people who work under you as employees, or even alongside you as colleagues, you have to treat them with mutual respect, even if they screw up.

And if you are a student, there is never a good excuse for bullying or name-calling. There's never an excuse for treating another student with jeers and insults, let alone inflicting physical harm. And remember that what may be a joke to you may be a damaging, harmful jab at someone else.

Here's the question:

Have you been a Jezebel to other people? Maybe because you are wealthier or more popular or have more privileges, or because you are able to work more and achieve more? Have you felt like you have license to treat others as lesser people?

What we learn from Ahab is that possessions are not more important than people. What we learn from Jezebel is that power is not more important than human dignity.

But there's an even more important lesson than either of those. It is this: you reap what you sow.

Ahab's Death

The nobles and elders, of course, carried out Jezebel's orders, and they put Naboth to death under false pretenses. Ahab got his vineyard after all. But when we get to the end of the story, we realize that Ahab and Jezebel eventually get what they deserve. They come to realize that you reap what you sow. What goes around comes around. The way you treat others, the way you live your life, will come back around to you someday.

And that's what happened to Ahab and Jezebel.

One day, Ahab was confronted by Elijah, who announced God's judgment and impending punishment on Ahab and Jezebel (1 Kings 21:20-24). Ahab, surprisingly, was penitent. God responded by showing Ahab mercy, postponing the judgment Elijah described instead of delivering it right away. But the sum total of Ahab's and Jezebel's sins, Naboth's vineyard included, caught up to them eventually. Neither Ahab nor Jezebel ever sought the Lord with their whole heart.

One day, Ahab took his army out to battle along with Jehoshaphat, king of Judah, to fight against the army of Aram. Despite being warned by a prophet of the Lord (not Elijah) that he would lose the battle, Ahab ignored the warning and went out to fight anyway. He put on a disguise so that the enemy couldn't see that he was the king. During the battle, he was killed, right there in his chariot, by an archer who didn't even know who he was. His comrades then took Ahab's body and hauled him, in the chariot, back to Israel. They buried him, and as they washed out his chariot, the water flowed into the pool of Samaria where dogs drank it. And so what God said to Elijah (1 Kings 21:19) came to pass after all: the dogs licked Ahab's blood (1 Kings 22:38). It's the Bible's way of saying that this wicked man suffered a dishonorable fate, which can happen to any of us who love possessions over people.

Now what about Jezebel? After Ahab's death, two of his sons reigned after him; Ahaziah ruled for two years and Joram ruled for twelve years. Jezebel continued to live in one of her palaces for fourteen years, continuing to treat others poorly, including her own servants. Then a man named Jehu, anointed by a prophet to be the new king, led an army and stormed Jezebel's palace (2 Kings 9). She was still so full of herself that even though she knew an army was coming to kill her, she sat in her room and put on makeup (2 Kings 9:30).

When Jehu stood outside below her room, on the second floor of the palace, he did a shrewd thing. He called out to all of Jezebel's servants and said, "Who's on my side? Anyone?" When a few people looked out the window, he told them to "throw her out!" (2 Kings 9:32-33).

The servants did as Jehu instructed, throwing Jezebel out of the window. Then she crashed on the ground and died. Earlier in the chapter, Jehu had killed Israel's king, Jezebel's son, and left him on a plot of ground that belonged to Naboth of Jezreel.

What goes around comes around. You cannot hide your indiscretions forever.

Jehu went in for a meal, then realized that Jezebel needed a decent burial, and when he came back, he saw that a pack of dogs had torn her piece by piece apart and nothing was left except her skull, hands, and feet. It's almost as if the mind that conceived her evils and her hands that carried them out were too evil even for the dogs to digest.

Payday, someday.

Do you treat possessions as more important than people? Are you exercising authority abusively over other people you are supposed to love? You need to know that you cannot live this way forever. What you sow you will reap.

Don't let the Ahab and the Jezebel within you prevail.

FINDING HOPE
IN HARD TIMES

What is preventing you from experiencing full contentment in the life you are currently living?

What would it take to let go of any temptation you have to put possessions over people?

How might you treat people in your life better, giving them the respect they deserve?

CHAPTER 3
WHEN LIFE TAKES A TURN

CHAPTER 3
WHEN LIFE TAKES A TURN

We have now hit the halfway point of our journey through the stories of Elijah and Elisha, and we are therefore at a critical moment in any multi-leg journey: the handoff. Relay racers can tell you that it's not only important to have speedy individual runners; the key to a successful race is in the hand off of the baton.

Think about Moses passing the baton to Joshua so the Israelites could enter the Promised Land. Or Solomon asking for wisdom when he assumed the throne from his father David. Or when John the Baptist prepared the way for Jesus to be the Savior of the world.

In your journey through hard times, you need to remember that you are not the only runner. You have been handed the baton by those who have run before you. And you are called to nurture the faithfulness of those who follow you. That's how hope is transferred: from one sojourner to the next, even when life takes a turn.

You Are Part of Something Bigger
2 Kings 2:1-18

In case you doubt it, here's a reminder: nobody lives forever. But this chapter is not about death.

And even though there are a few exceptions to this rule, here is another reminder: nobody stays in the same place forever. But this chapter is not about good-byes.

No, instead, this is about perspective. It is about remembering that the work of God's kingdom is bigger than any one person, no matter how great that person might be. It's also about remembering that even though you might feel like a small and insignificant part of God's kingdom, you are, in fact, a critical part of what God wants to do in the world.

God's kingdom is bigger than you imagined. And so is your role in it.

At the beginning of this Scripture passage, the narrator tells us that Elijah was traveling down the home stretch of his life. He would soon be departing from this earth, leaving behind quite a legacy. He would be regarded as one of the most successful, most powerful, and most influential prophets in the history of the Israelite people. And we would be right to wonder how the work of God would continue after he was gone.

You can see the doubt in the story. On two separate occasions the observers, the other prophets, pressed Elisha, Elijah's successor, with the question: "Do you know that the LORD is going to take your master away from you today?" (2 Kings 2:3, 5). What they were really asking was, "What in the world is going to happen to the ministry now? How are you going to fill such big shoes?"

What these people, these prophets even, failed to recognize, and what this story teaches us, is that the kingdom is bigger than any one individual, and the work of God continues without fail.

The same is true for each of us Christians. When one of us is weak, we can depend on someone around us for strength. When one of us is grieving, we can turn to someone around us for comfort. And when one of us is in need, we should always be able to turn to a fellow Christian for help. The kingdom of God is built on relationships, friendships, and connections bigger than any one individual.

This chapter is not about death or good-byes. It is not about Elijah's departure or Elisha's promotion. It is about connection. It is a reminder that each of us is an integral part of an intricate connection of people who depend on one another for spiritual growth and Christian action.

At one point on the journey, Elijah turned to Elisha and asked him the question: "What do you want me to do for you before I'm taken away from you?" (2 Kings 2:9). What is one thing I can do for you before I leave?

Elisha's answer was as poignant as it was cryptic: "Let me have twice your spirit" (verse 9). Or as another translation puts it, "Let me inherit a double share of your spirit" (NRSV).

Elisha was referring to the traditional practice of bestowing inheritances upon the next generation. In Israelite culture, traditionally the oldest son would receive a "double portion" of the father's estate when he died. In other words, the oldest son would get twice as much as his brothers. In Elijah's case, Elisha was not a blood relative, but a spiritual one, and the bequest was not material, but sacred. For his inheritance, Elisha was asking for a double share of Elijah's spiritual authority, his divine power, and his calling from God—which doesn't necessarily mean twice Elijah's spirit, just a greater share than that of the other prophets. In other words, Elisha wanted to be recognized as the prophetic equivalent of Elijah's firstborn. He was asking for Elijah's blessing to continue the work that God was doing.

So here is the invitation for you and me. What is it that your ancestors have left for you to continue in your work? I'm not talking professionally, of course, though you may be involved in a career that continues your family business. This is about your spiritual work, the work that God has entrusted to you to make this world a better place.

A good place to start would be in thinking about all those who have played a role in introducing you to the faith and strengthening your discipleship journey. You might think of a family member, a spiritual mentor, or a close friend.

When I think about those kinds of people in my life, I always begin with my parents.

My father, Maghirang deVega, was born in the Philippines in the 1940s in a city called Cavite, just outside metropolitan Manila. He graduated from a Filipino university and started a career as a high school teacher when he began to imagine the prospects of getting married and starting a family.

As a young adult, he realized he had to make a choice. He thought that in order to give his future children the best chance at the best possible life, he would need to leave his impoverished life in the Philippines for a better life in the United States. So, that's what he did.

He left for America in the late 1960s to find work, promising to return someday for my mother, then his girlfriend, in order for them to get married. For several long months, with just a few dollars in his pocket, my dad crisscrossed the country, riding a Greyhound bus from San Diego, California, to Miami, Florida, looking for employment. He had barely enough money to afford Baby Ruth candy bars from the bus station vending machines, his only subsistence for his cross-country trip. Finally, he earned a job as a chemical engineer in St. Petersburg, Florida.

As for his relationship with my mother, because of his limited funds, my parents could not afford long-distance telephone calls between the U.S. and the Philippines, and mail delivery was quite unreliable. So, for four long years, as my dad earned U.S. citizenship and established his new life here, they could not communicate a single time.

Yet, they waited for each other. And true to his word, when my father became a U.S. citizen, he went back to the Philippines for my mother, and they were married in the United States. A year later, they gave birth to me.

Shortly after my birth, my parents and I were living in a simple, suburban apartment complex in Ft. Lauderdale, Florida. One day, my dad did an amazing thing with me. On a bright, clear morning, my dad picked me up out of my crib and took me outside, into the commons area of the apartment complex. He walked with me in his arms to a gazebo. And there, in the privacy of that moment, he lifted me up to the sky. He looked up to God and into my sweet little face and he said a prayer to God.

> O Lord, you gave him to me. I am dedicating
> him back to you. Use him, but you will have to
> provide him with the talents that he will need to
> serve you. Use him in any way you want to, in any
> field, be it in academics, music, art, or athletics, as
> long as he does it to glorify you.

He offered me to God, and said that my life belonged to God's purpose and plan. He uttered some simple, powerful words, not knowing then how that moment would shape my life and my future career. But when I told him back in 1995 that I was no longer interested in being a doctor, but wanted to pursue a career in ministry, he remembered that moment in the apartment gazebo. And it was then and there that it all made sense to him.

When I think about the Elijahs in my life, I think about my father, the one who taught me about loyalty, honesty, hard work, and putting your family first, above all else. But most of all, he was the one who set within me the foundation for a life of faith.

I also think about my mother's father, my grandfather. He died when I was a teenager, and he didn't speak much English. But we would spend lots of my childhood days fishing together and sharing our favorite TV show, which transcended human language: *The Three Stooges*. I have never known a more hardworking, gentle, and contented man in my life. If I were to receive a double portion of his spirit, I would live my days with the same kind of determination, the same kind of gentle spirit, and the same kind of reverence for life and others. And I try to do just that, every day.

I think about my second-grade teacher, Ruth Ferrell, who first taught me about Jesus Christ, with a kind of kindness and grace that made the story of Christ's love so endearing and so enduring. If I were to receive a double portion of her spirit, I would do the same for others, proclaiming Christ's message without judgment and with great love for others. And that's what I try to do, every day.

And I think about my spiritual ancestors who are still alive, who can still share with me lessons of the faith. I think of the pastor of my childhood church, which was the setting of my call into ministry, who taught me about keeping up with my studies and taught me to never stop learning. I think about my aunt, who prays for me with an earnest, diligent spirit, and teaches me to pray in the same way.

The point is that each one of us has an Elijah in our past, from whom we receive the example and the capacity to continue the spiritual work of the kingdom in our lives. Who is it that you can learn from? Who are those people in your past to whom you have said good-bye, but who can live on in your actions and your example? Maybe it is a parent or grandparent, a dear friend or neighbor, a pastor, coworker, or loved one. Know that they continue to live on, just as Elijah lived on through the work of Elisha. They can live on through you.

But there's more to the story. As Elisha saw the fiery chariot and horses with Elijah soaring into the clouds, keeping his eye on his ascent in that windstorm, symbolically pledging to keep his mentor's work in his field of vision forever, Elijah indeed imparted that double portion of his spirit on his life.

Elisha's first act was to take the mantle, the outer cloak of Elijah, and to strike the waters of the Jordan. To everyone's amazement, the waters parted before him, just as they had when Elijah struck the water in the same way. At that moment, Elisha knew that the power of Elijah was transferred on him. And he also realized that the roles were now reversed. Just as Elijah had been a mentor and friend to him, he would now need to be the same for someone else.

No, today's story is not about death, and it's not about good-byes. Instead, it's about connection. And it is about perspective. It is about seeing your life as the sum result of those whose spiritual influences brought you to this point. It is about remembering that it is your turn, your responsibility to pass on that mantle to others.

So, who are you going to raise in the faith? Who are you going to serve and mentor in the way that guides them, directs them, and models for them a life of holiness? Will it be a family member? Or maybe a person in your church? Or a coworker who is seeking hope or a neighbor who is hurting?

Every day, as you live your life, notice who walks alongside you. There are always two people. The first is your Elijah, who influences each of your steps and shows you the path to follow. The second is your Elisha, who is watching you, learning from you, and wanting to emulate how you think, act, and respond.

How is that for some perspective?

When Words Hurt
2 Kings 2:23-25

We've heard the old adage, "Sticks and stones may break my bones, but words will never hurt me." And we've lived long enough to know how untrue that saying is. Words do hurt. In some ways, they hurt worse than sticks and stones, because they cut us at a deeper level than just the skin and bones.

Has there ever been a time when someone's words hurt you in a way you still remember to this day? Are the wounds still as fresh

FINDING HOPE
IN HARD TIMES

Who have been the Elijahs of your life?

How might you express your gratitude for the influence they have been for you?

Who are the Elishas of your life?

How might you better carry out your responsibility to model the faith for them?

and open now as when you were first injured? Might there even be a time when you were the word-thrower? when your emotions consumed you with such ferocity that you erupted with a verbal assault that felt right at the time, but you might admit caused lasting damage in your relationship?

Words do hurt. And the wounds that come from them don't heal quickly.

Elisha surely learned that lesson in the story from 2 Kings 2:23-25. It's a story that is very different in plot and tone from all the other stories about Elijah and Elisha. Here, the conflict is not staged with fire on an altar, a wind in a cave, ravens by a brook, or oil in a widow's pantry. It involves the simplest and most intangible weapon of all: the spoken word.

It actually begins before that, in verses 15-18. Elisha, having just experienced a remarkable, life-transforming moment of transition, took up the mantle of Elijah's power and responsibility. You and I would be filled with anticipation and excitement, just as he must have been in spite of the sadness he also surely felt now that Elijah was gone. And just like that, the shoe dropped, as misfortune was lurking just around the corner.

Right after he scooped up the mantle and wrung it dry from its miraculous river-parting, he was suddenly greeted by a crowd of prophets, including fifty strong men. They were former servants of his predecessor Elijah, and they had not seen what had just happened to their master. They were convinced that he was still around, that God had picked him up and deposited him far away, and they came storming up to Elisha looking for answers.

And when Elisha tried to explain to them the truth, that Elijah was not hiding from them but was in fact gone for good, they would have nothing of it. They insisted that they be allowed to go and look for him. To Elisha it must have felt like a vote of no confidence in him; they were doubting his word, and they wanted to do everything in their power to restore their former master, Elijah. They persisted in their request to Elisha "until he became embarrassed" (2 Kings 2:17).

Words really do hurt.

Before we go much further, pause for a moment and think about how jarring a moment that had to be for Elisha, just as it is for us. How many times in your life have you had a "mountaintop" experience, where all felt right and you experienced deep peace and responsibility, only to be greeted the next day, or even the next moment, with news that sank your spirits back to the ground?

I've had more than enough of those in my life, really. In fact, that sudden drop from high to low has happened so many times that for a long while, I couldn't fully appreciate those joyous moments out of a fearful conviction that something bad was bound to happen next. It became so debilitating that I began to believe that even allowing myself to feel joy *prompted* the counterbalance of sadness to come.

You might not have ever gotten to that extreme, or maybe you have. Either way, maybe you can identify with times in your life when you felt like the rough times were entirely deserved, as if you were the one who prompted the bad news yourself. It's a rough way to live, huh?

One thing that helped was a series of sessions with my therapist, who has been and continues to be a great gift to me. After I explained my thought processes, how I connected moments of joy with subsequent moments of sadness—sharing all this with a certain degree of embarrassment—she offered this therapeutic exercise.

She asked me to take an index card, a pen, and a pair of scissors, and to keep them handy. The next time something good was followed by something bad, she told me to write down the good experience at the top of the card, and the bad experience at the bottom. She told me to close my eyes, offer a prayer, then use the scissors to cut apart the top and bottom of the card. It would be a way of symbolically and psychologically separating the good and bad experiences, as a reminder that despite my brain's efforts to create a cause-and-effect relationship between the two, they were not related. I could therefore feel free to enjoy the fullness of the highs of my life without fear. And I could also feel free to experience the depth of the sad times of my life, without guilt that I always deserved it.

I'll admit that I thought this was a silly exercise at first. But given how much I trust my therapist, I tried it. I set out an index card, a pen, and a pair of scissors in a visible place in my house— my kitchen counter—and kept these at the ready for when I needed them. For weeks, I passed by that counter and looked at those items, thinking about what they represented to me.

And do you know what? I've never done the exercise. It's not because I think it's silly, and it's not because good times have never since been followed by bad. They inevitably have, many times since I set out those items. But looking at that card, pen, and scissors every day eventually drilled into my brain the deeper truth: there is no cause-and-effect relationship between highs and lows. The universe doesn't punish me for relishing the moment. Nor am I to hedge my heart and disable it from feeling pain, sadness, glee, or contentment. It's not only okay to feel; it's important to do so. Because that's what makes us human.

This brings us back to Elisha. There he was, having experienced a remarkable high in his life, and he was immediately greeted by his fellow prophets, who were convinced that Elisha wasn't telling them the truth about what happened to Elijah. They doubted his word and his leadership. And even after the men came back from a fruitless, three-day search that failed to find Elijah, his troubles were not over.

In verses 23-25, a group of young people took their turn hurling insults. In this case, it had to do with his follicularly-challenged head. They called him "baldy." But it wasn't just his bald head they were insulting. They said, "Get going, Baldy! Get going, Baldy!" (verse 23), which was another way of saying, "Get out of here! You're not welcome!" It's as if they were saying to him, "You are a complete alien to this place! You are not one of us! Go back to whatever planet, foreign land, or group of weirdos you came from!" And they topped it off by insulting his appearance.

Their insult about his bald head was wrapped up in a deeper insult. They were insulting his identity, his dignity, his humanity. That was a whole lot worse.

Indeed, that's when words hurt the most: when people insult the deepest part of who we are; when they do more than demoralize—they dehumanize; when they refuse to acknowledge the humanity of a person, as if someone doesn't deserve to breathe the same air as everyone else.

I don't know if you've ever been cut to that level with someone else's words. If so, you may never forget it.

The temptation, of course, is to lash back, to return insult with insult, injury with injury, and to cleanse our hurt souls of rage by channeling it with return fire. And in fact, Elisha did respond.

In verse 24, Elisha, the newly minted mouthpiece for God, the prophet with a message for the world, responded in a way that was far from saintly. He cursed them back, in the name of the Lord. And while the Bible doesn't specifically say that he called up the two bears that tore the forty-two youths into pieces, we can safely assume that Elisha was responsible.

We're left to wrestle with Elisha's response. We can either raise it up in virtue as a model response, or we can treat it as a negative example to learn from. Indeed, there are times when it is right to stay firm, respond in anger, and react with righteous indignation to injustice. Sometimes, it is okay to burn with a white-hot holy anger when people are being mistreated and oppression rules the day.

There are lots of examples of that kind of response in the Bible, and this very well may be one of them.

But we can also remember the exponentially greater number of examples in the Bible when reacting in such a way is not God's prescription, when the hard work of peace is the way to follow, and we are called to seek justice through nonviolent means.

Jesus, after all, calls us to bless those who curse us and pray for those who persecute us (Matthew 5:44). James calls us to be quick to listen and slow to anger and to bridle our tongues (James 1:19; 3:2-12). Paul commands us to be angry but not sin, and to not let the sun go down on our anger (Ephesians 4:26-27).

The trick, of course, is to know how to use our words to heal rather than hurt. Because for every instance when we would want to summon the bears against our attackers, God may be calling us to forge a pathway to peace, understanding, and forgiveness.

Making Peace by Building Trust

My friend Gary Mason works with an international peace-making group called Rethinking Conflict, traveling around the world into places of conflict and working to build new bridges of understanding, reconciliation, and peace. He is from Northern Ireland, which was plagued by a civil war not long ago, a war that lasted over thirty years. It split the country into two warring factions: the Unionists, predominantly Protestant, who were primarily loyal to England, and the Nationalists, predominantly Catholic, who found their primary identity with Ireland. Over that time, 3,500 men and women were killed and thousands more injured, in a war that is now popularly termed "The Troubles."

The Troubles ended in 1998 with a peace agreement that effectively put an end to the atrocities. But the process of making peace was just beginning, for peace is not merely the absence of conflict. It is a commitment to the hard work of transforming the human heart.

In October 2017, I spent a week with Gary in Belfast with about eighteen fellow clergy. He reminded us that "even though there was an end to violence with a gun, there remained violence with the tongue." That peace would take longer. But thanks to earnest people from both sides of the conflict, it is a peace that is slowly developing.

Two such individuals are Sean Murray and Winston Irvine, who were on opposite sides of the war. Sean was a Nationalist and

Winston a Unionist, each man trained to kill the other during the height of the war.

One of the most stirring moments of our trip was to see these two men, now twenty years after the end of the conflict, not only in the same room together, and not only sitting next to each other, but talking to each other and calling each other friend.

They once embodied global conflict, and now they embody the possibility of global peace. It's all because they first experienced peace within their hearts and learned how to empathize with the story of the other person.

They came to the realization that their own personal perspective was not the only valid one. Winston at one point said, "We came to realize that there was not one narrative. There were many ways to see the same situation, and when we came to that understanding, there was a breakthrough."

Sean admitted that the peace agreement settled the conflict on a macro level, but the process of rebuilding and unifying the country requires leadership and trust. So now, twenty years later, Sean can say, "I respect Winston's point of view, and he respects mine. We may not agree, but we can see through the other's eyes."

Wouldn't it be nice to be able to say that in the major divisions and polarizing issues of our day? Wouldn't it be nice to say to someone with whom you have stark disagreements: *I respect the other person's point of view, and the other person respects mine. We may not agree, but we can see through the other's eyes.*

Oh, I know that's hard. In fact, someone in our group asked them: "How is that possible? How can you possibly empathize with someone who thinks so little of you, even with hatred in their

FINDING HOPE
IN HARD TIMES

How have you been hurt by someone else's words in the past?

How have you hurt someone else?

What can you do to begin the process of healing, based on empathy and a mutual affirmation of each other's dignity and worth?

hearts for you? Let alone the hatred you might have for them and their perspective?"

To which Winston offered this: "In the early days of engagement, there was a huge amount of mistrust and it took time to learn each other's stories. There were some hurtful conversations, but you don't have to agree with someone to understand them. Trust is built when people see words translated into action . . . dialogue makes people human. The first order of war is to dehumanize them, and it makes it easier to kill them. The first order of peace is to humanize the other person, and that is what builds up trust. Along the way, we have to ask, 'What is the cost if we don't? What is the cost if we don't engage the other person?'"

As we heard them and watched them together, the best way to describe what we were witnessing was wonder.

Yes, words hurt. But they can also heal. How might you participate in the reconciling of a broken relationship or warring people or even the conflicted emotional responses you feel within yourself?

Keep Pouring
2 Kings 4:1-7

It is sometimes said, "History doesn't repeat itself, but it does echo." It's a statement we might apply to this story from 2 Kings, as it sounds awfully similar to the one in 1 Kings 17. The difference, of course, is that this is Elisha, not Elijah. And this is a widow from among the company of prophets, not of Zarephath. But so many of the key elements are here: poverty, hopelessness, and a little jar of oil that God somehow replenished to meet her need.

The widow had been married to a colleague of Elisha, a member of the group of prophets. And when her husband died, she was left with a heap of trouble. Not only was she left with little opportunity for income, for which she had depended on her husband, she was also left with an incredible amount of debt due to money he had borrowed. We're not told where that debt came from; we are only told that it was too large for this woman to take care of on her own. And, perhaps worst of all, the creditors came knocking. Because she didn't have the money, the woman faced the possibility that her children would be sold into slavery in order to pay off the debt.

Put yourself in this woman's shoes. She was grieving the loss of her husband, saddled with a debt she could not pay, and scared to death that she might lose her children. We learn all of this in one verse, and it leaves us breathless.

If ever a person in the Bible needed a miracle, it was this widow.

It does beckon the question of what we believe about miracles today. What do we mean when we speak of miracles? Do we believe in them? How do we pray for them? If we were in this woman's shoes, would we ask God to provide one? What is a miracle, anyway? Are miracles fact or fiction?

It is a question we might have been asking all along throughout this journey through the stories of Elijah and Elisha. After all, we have heard some amazing stories. We've read about fire raining down from the sky, ravens bringing food along rivers, and children being raised from the dead. These stories have had all the marks of a summer blockbuster movie, complete with special effects, stunning plot twists, and unbelievable endings. And we would be right to wonder whether these stories are little more than Hollywood fiction.

What are we to do with these miracle stories? It's more than a question of how we *interpret* these stories—as literal, historical fact, or as metaphor. The deeper question is how these stories might shape our understanding of God, ourselves, and our relationship with God today.

That's what we might explore in this story. What would it mean to experience a miracle from God today?

Again, if we were the poor widow, we might assume that the only kind of miracle we should expect is if God were to do something like rain money down from the sky. Or if all the creditors, for some unforeseen reason, decided to forgive the debt. Or if the woman somehow won the Hebrew Powerball lottery.

None of those things happened. But a miracle still did occur. And it is the kind of miracle we can expect today. Maybe our task is to redefine what miracles might mean today, in a way that opens us up beyond our limited views of how God can and might operate in our lives.

First, this miracle required the woman's participation. She was to be not a passive recipient of God's miracle but an active participant in it. Elisha told her to take an inventory of what she had in her home, in which she found only a jar of oil. She would pour the oil according to Elisha's instructions. For this miracle to occur, the woman would have to play a role herself.

Second, this miracle required a community willing to come to her side. Not only would she have to act, she would need to rely on the help of others. And those others, for their part, would have to step up and come to her aid. She would have to ask her neighbors for the chance to borrow vessels of all shapes and sizes. Large urns, medium-sized pots, small cups. Any kind of container needed to be brought into her home. Each vessel symbolized the care and concern of someone who wanted to do her or his part to help this woman.

With as many containers collected as possible, Elisha told the woman and her sons to go in the room with the vessels, close the door, and begin pouring. And when the woman poured that little bit of oil into the first vessel, there was enough to fill it. So she kept on pouring, into the second vessel. And then into the third and fourth. All the way until the very last vessel that they had collected was filled.

Finally, this miracle brought blessing to others as well. She was not going to be the only one receiving the full benefits of the miracle for herself. Because of her willingness to participate, and because of the community coming by her side, a miracle was done not only to her but through her. The Bible says that all of the oil that came out of that little jar into all those containers could be sold, and the money used to pay off her debts, and she could save her children. I like to think this miracle brought the woman and all of her neighbors together. And I like to think the people she sold the oil to also received the blessing that God had miraculously provided through the oil.

In the Bible, when a miracle happens it is often not simply for the sole benefit of the person receiving a miracle. Often it occurs so that other people can receive a miracle through that person.

So, do miracles happen today? Yes, they do. And maybe not always in the way you think. When we are open to them, actively participate in them, come together as a community to make them happen, and seek to change the world from them, miracles can and will happen.

Here's just one example.

In 1942, a Christian author named Clarence Jordan and his wife were so gripped by the rampant racism and moral decay of the Deep South that they decided to form a new kind of community. It was called the Koinonia Farm in the town of Americus, Georgia. They held together some central values as the ones that would guide their community: Treat all human beings with dignity and justice. Choose love over violence. Share all possessions and live simply. Be stewards of the land and its natural resources.

In 1963, Millard and Linda Fuller visited friends at Koinonia Farm during a family vacation. They began a relationship with Clarence Jordan that ultimately led to the creation of Habitat for Humanity.

Jordan espoused an expression of Christianity that motivated him and the Fullers to seek ways to express God's love to their poorer neighbors. Koinonia Farm became Koinonia Partners in 1969 as the small community undertook several new projects, the primary focus of which was Partnership Housing. Believing that what the poor needed was capital, not charity, Jordan and Millard Fuller, along with other members of the Koinonia community, planned to develop a revolving "Fund for Humanity" that would take in donations that would be used to purchase building materials. Volunteer laborers would construct simple, decent houses along with the families who would eventually own the houses. The homeowners would then repay the cost of the materials to the Fund for Humanity at zero interest. In this way, the work was not a giveaway program and the funds repaid were then used to begin work on additional houses.

Since then, Habitat for Humanity has emerged as an independent organization and is still going strong, building hundreds of thousands of houses around the world.

FINDING HOPE
IN HARD TIMES

What do you think about miracles? Is there any barrier that prevents you from believing in them?

Might there be a different way for you to think about them?

Most importantly, how might God be calling you to participate in someone else's miracle?

Now, I would call that a miracle.

Our belief in miracles is a central part of what it means to be a person of faith. It's not because we need to check our brains at the door and not because it is impossible to be both an intellectual person and a person of faith. It's because believing in the impossible makes things possible. These stories expand our vision of the way things might be.

If we open ourselves up to the idea of oil being inexhaustible, or bread and fish being multiplied for a crowd, or a dead person being raised to life, then maybe we will open ourselves up to some other incredible ideas too.

Like the idea that our economic system can and should support the poorest and most needy.

Like the idea that an excess of material possessions can be burdensome and even dangerous.

Like the idea that peace is possible, and that international relationships can claim cooperation, rather than competition, as a value.

And maybe, in the same way that Elisha embraced widows and Jesus embraced outcasts, we are not only allowed but expected to cross every boundary to welcome every identity at this table.

In a world where revenge is the norm and forgiveness is the exception, maybe the miracle that drives us is the belief in the irrational decision to follow the example of Jesus Christ.

Maybe the Resurrection is not only a miracle to be believed but also a life to be lived and a way of life for community to live together.

Once we start believing in miracles, there is no telling just where it may lead us.

CHAPTER 4
WHEN ALL SEEMS LOST

CHAPTER 4
WHEN ALL SEEMS LOST

Most good novels and films have an "all is lost" moment. It's that point in the plot when the hero or heroine hits the lowest point in their entire journey, when their desired outcome seems too far to be achieved. Those moments are not just useful plot devices for setting up the climax and resolution. They are gateways for us, the reader and audience, to enter the hero's journey with our own similar "all is lost" moments.

We've all been there, when the darkness seems at its thickest and hope seems at its most elusive. It's when we feel most afraid, most helpless, and least able to go another step.

Each of these final stories in the life of Elisha tracks through some of the toughest "all is lost" moments we go through. But in each case, we discover that night is always darkest before dawn, as the old saying goes. And hope is closer than you think.

When It Looks Like Death Has Won
2 Kings 4:8-37

This story is almost a reverse image of the previous one. Instead of a poor widow, Elisha meets a rich benefactress. Instead of meeting a family in distress, Elisha meets a family of means. And instead of Elisha arriving to solve a problem, he comes to receive a blessing.

It is a family with whom Elisha had a history of regular pleasantries. When he happened to be in the area, he would stop by for a visit. When he was hungry, they would always have something to feed him. When he was tired, they'd put him up for the night. He became such a frequent guest in their home that the woman and her husband decided to do the highly unusual thing and build him his own separate living area. His very own room, on his very own floor, on the roof of the house.

What a generous couple.

And Elisha knew it. One day, sitting in his comfortable digs and relishing the good fortune of knowing such a generous family, he started talking to his servant about some way to thank them for all they had done for him. What do you give a family who has everything?

When asked, the woman said she had found contentment already in her life. There was nothing that she needed, as she had the only things that really mattered to her, a home to live in and a spouse to live with. Anything beyond that was extra blessing.

Maybe that is why Elisha stopped by for a visit as regularly as he did. Perhaps it wasn't just because he was greeted so warmly with a hot meal and a comfortable bed, and not just because they did the audacious thing and built him his own guest suite. Maybe it was because this couple had found and exhibited one of the most elusive qualities in the human condition, something that many people strive for a lifetime to achieve but never attain: a feeling of contentment. Elisha might have found that to be so remarkable that he wanted to be in their presence as often as he could.

Wouldn't you?

Still, Elisha wanted to thank them. He wanted to do something for them that they could not do for themselves. But what could he do?

Well, his servant Gehazi said, they don't have a child.

Infertility is a common theme throughout the Scriptures: Abraham and Sarah in Genesis, Hannah in 1 Samuel, Zechariah and Elizabeth in Luke. If you or someone you know has had this struggle, then you are not alone. The Bible offers you solidarity and camaraderie in your sorrow, and it reminds you that God has always demonstrated a special compassion for those unable to have biological children.

Elisha immediately jumped on the idea. Like God's message to Abraham and Sarah, and Gabriel's annunciation to Mary, Elisha's declaration to this remarkable couple proclaimed that in a year's time, they would have a son. And after a year, they did.

Then years later, after the boy had learned to walk and speak, tragedy struck. With no warning or explanation from the biblical text, the child experienced some kind of traumatic head condition, prompting him to run to his father in pain and be carried to his mother in anguish.

And within a short time, he died (verse 20).

We would be hard-pressed to find any other couple who lived quite as much a roller coaster of emotions in such a short amount of time as this couple from Shunem. They went from contented, affable people, to overjoyed new parents, to heartbroken and bewildered couple all within a few years. They had everything they needed, then got something they always wanted, and then felt like they lost everything that mattered.

The mother, desolate with grief, then paid an emergency visit to Elisha, in which she grabbed his feet—a sign of pleading and likely also of sorrow—and clutched him so tightly that Gehazi assumed she was intending harm. But Elisha waved him aside and listened to the woman say these words:

"Did I ask you for a son, sir? Didn't I say, 'Don't raise my hopes'?" (2 Kings 4:28).

It's hard to determine exactly the tone of the woman's voice. We could read distress in those words, or maybe anger, or maybe numbness. Regardless, she was working through her grief by naming the fact that as much a blessing as having a child had been, life was simpler before he was born.

The woman's words, heartbreak and all, remind us of this important characteristic of life. When something goes from simplicity to complexity—whether it be a family, a community, or a system of any kind—then it increases its capacity for beauty and goodness, as well as the possibility for sorrow and chaos.

Look at your own life. Chances are good that when you were a child, you had fewer relationships and responsibilities than you do now. Life was simpler. And while there were fewer rewards, there were also fewer risks. But as you grew older, expanding your abilities and your networks of friendships, you increased your capacity for love, harmony, and beauty. But with it has come a commensurate amount of sadness, loss, and suffering.

The woman, in her grief, flashed back to a simpler time, before the grief, before the birth of her son, and before the prophet Elisha gave her something she never asked for, even though it was something she really wanted.

If you are going through a hard time in your life right now, is there a part of you that thinks the same way as this woman did?

If only I could go back in time, when life was not this hard.

If only I could reset my relationship with that person who hurt me, and choose to live a simpler, more isolated life.

If only I had chosen a career that wasn't as demanding, or had a family that was not so complicated, or could maybe even return to a time when my faith was so much more childlike and innocent. Before the doubts that I cannot shake, before the questions I cannot answer, before the mysteries I cannot solve on my own.

In a way, the Shunammite woman was asking Elisha, "Why couldn't you have let me live the simpler life I was living before?"

The answer to that question is that life is not always that way. It is the ambiguity and complexity of existence that characterize the rich and full life, while a lack of complications belongs to a one-dimensional life. Just as light creates shadows, life is a constant interplay between mourning and dancing, blessing and persecution, a time to weep and a time to laugh, as it says in Ecclesiastes.

We can also imagine an even deeper, more painful undertone to the woman's words. Not only was she grieving her son's death, she was haunted by the notion that Elisha and God had failed her. She had to be thinking, "Okay, God. You promised you would show up, but you didn't. What gives? Are you even around?"

In this respect, she's like the disciples in the Gospels who were on the boat as the waves were crashing and the storm was tossing, and Jesus was nowhere to be found. She's like Mary and Martha, who were certain that their brother Lazarus would not have died if Jesus had just shown up according to plan. She's even like Jesus himself, who wondered why God had abandoned him on the cross. Maybe she's also like Elijah, who had presumed to find God in the wind, fire, and earthquake on Mount Horeb, only to find God hidden, somehow, in the place God was least likely to be found.

The woman was asking a question many of us have asked at some point in our lives: Where is God when it hurts?

"Did I ask you for a son, sir? Didn't I say, 'Don't raise my hopes'?"

Elisha's response to the woman's question was immediate and decisive. He told his servant, "Get ready, take my staff, and go! If you encounter anyone, don't stop to greet them. If anyone greets you, don't reply. Put my staff on the boy's face" (2 Kings 4:29).

But the woman would have nothing of it. She wanted nothing less than the prophet, not his servant Gehazi, to pay her son a visit.

But Gehazi ran ahead of them, and when he attempted to follow Elisha's prescription and placed the staff on the boy, it failed. If it troubled the woman or Elisha to hear this news, we can't be sure, but we know we would be disappointed.

So Elisha decided that rather than use some kind of inanimate object to bring about healing, he would offer the most deeply personal resource he had: the sense of his own touch, the presence of his own breath, the gift of his whole being.

After a prayer, he leaned over the boy's body, eye to eye, face to face, hand to hand. And then the boy's core temperature started to rise, air started to fill his nostrils, and a sneezing fit overtook him as his lifeless body sputtered back to life.

Then Elisha called for his servant and said, "Call the Shunammite woman." Tell his mom . . . there is good news here.

And when the woman arrived, presumably with tears of joy and cries of relief, she picked up her son and left.

We don't hear much about this woman again. She and Elisha met briefly once more in 2 Kings 8, but then she went away for seven years. We might assume she and Elisha saw each other after that. Or maybe they never spoke again. But we can safely assume one thing: her life was never the same. This woman, who had learned contentment when her life was simpler, learned to turn with confidence and boldness to God when her life was at its most complicated and chaotic. And that insight, even more than the gift of the birth of her son or his being raised from the dead, might be the greatest gift she received from this whole episode.

God wants you to find contentment and gratitude, no matter what stage of life you are in. That's awfully hard to find sometimes, especially when all seems lost and God seems nowhere to be found. But just like this woman was tenacious in her conviction that only Elisha himself could be the one to turn this story around, just as she would settle for nothing less, sometimes the best thing we can do is to grab hold of God's feet. To refuse to shake loose, no matter what the odds are telling us. Because somehow, in some way, we need to trust that God can do the impossible, even when it feels much too complicated.

And do you know what? God can.

FINDING HOPE
IN HARD TIMES

Do you sometimes ruefully wish you could go back to a time in your life when things were simpler?

Even though life might be more complicated for you now, what benefit has going through these tough times brought you?

How has it strengthened your faith?

Healing for Deeper Hurts
2 Kings 5:1-19

Humpty Dumpty sat on a wall
Humpty Dumpty had a great fall
And all the king's horses and all the king's men
Couldn't put Humpty together again

Here is what we know. Eggs don't belong on walls. And when one breaks, it is impossible to put it back together.

But the nursery rhyme reminds us of this deeper truth about the human condition. When the mighty fall, there is nothing in this world that can bring true healing. Whether this poem is originally about King Richard III in the fifteenth century or English weapons of war in the seventeenth century, it is a reminder of this universal truth: if we depend on human strength and might alone, then human pride will always stand in the way of true healing.

But there is one thing we can discover that can bring true healing and wholeness to the broken places in our own lives, and in the broken systems of this world. It's found in this episode from the ministry of Elisha.

If you want to know what it is, just ask the military commander named Naaman. He was a commanding officer in the army of Aram, an enemy to the Israelites. He was a powerful person, of significant influence, with an array of soldiers and servants at his constant disposal. He was like a five-star general in the army of Aram, a powerful nation that had received victory and might in large part through Naaman's leadership.

This was no ordinary man, but he had an ordinary disease. He was fighting a skin disease that had no cure, and if it was serious he may have been staring at a death sentence.

This Ancient Near Eastern Humpty Dumpty had a great fall, and he was desperate for a cure. So, he tried to assemble all the king's horses and all the king's men to see if they could come up with a solution.

The first person to offer help was his wife's Israelite servant girl, whom he had captured during one of his raids on Israel. The servant girl suggested that Naaman should go to the Lord's prophet in Israel. This would have been a controversial move, and it could have been done only if Naaman's king, the king of Aram, agreed. This would have been like the president of the United States sending one of our army generals over to North Korea for medical help. Some things are just too preposterous to consider!

But the king of Aram agreed, and Naaman was on his way to Israel to look for a cure. And in true Humpty Dumpty fashion, Naaman rolled in with all the king's horses and all the king's men, in an impressive show of bravado and pride: 750 pounds of silver, 150 pounds of gold, and at least ten full sets of clothing. Such a treasure would be worth around $3 million by today's standards. The message to the helpless king of Israel is simple: heal him and get a nice tidy little sum—don't heal him and we'll dump the treasure, wipe out your army, and then go home.

Israel's king, predictably, panicked. With Naaman's imposing forces marching closer and closer to Israel, there seemed to be a threat of battle with just the slightest misstep. The king ripped his clothes in anguish at the difficulty of his situation.

Elisha, however, heard about the king's reaction and sent word to him. "Let the man come to me," Elisha wrote. "Then he'll know that there's a prophet in Israel" (2 Kings 5:8).

Naaman was on his way to Elisha's house with his horses and chariots, and all the suspense was built up for a high-stakes, politically-charged confrontation. All Naaman wanted was healing... but he had no idea just how much healing he really needed. And he was utterly unprepared for what happened next.

You see, what was really broken about Naaman was not his skin but his pride. He thought his power alone could afford him anything he thought he was entitled to, and he believed that he was a self-made, self-preserved man. If he had a problem with his skin, it was that it was too thin, just like Humpty Dumpty's shell. Silver, gold, clothes, and the threat of military might ought to fix things just fine.

He was a prideful man. And while God was in fact concerned about the disease on his skin, God was even more concerned about the disease in his soul.

So what Elisha did to Naaman was absolutely, hilariously rich. With Naaman standing there outside Elisha's house, chariots and all, you could almost sense Naaman's chest puffed with pride, when he called for Elisha to come out.

Then he waited. And he waited.

The door creaked open, and out came... not Elisha. Instead, it was Elisha's messenger. And he delivered a simple message. "Go and wash seven times in the Jordan River. Then your skin will be restored and become clean" (2 Kings 5:10).

Elisha won't be seeing you personally, but asks that you take seven dips in the river and call him in the morning. Thank you! Bye-bye.

And Naaman went berserk.

His exact reaction recorded in the Bible was this: "I thought that for me he would surely come out!" (verse 11 NRSV).

It was further confirmation of what Naaman's biggest problem was. He wasn't worried about the skin disease because of the physical problems it would cause. He was concerned about the skin disease because of what it would do to his reputation. This was a man who had built a career based on charisma and who guarded his life with external projections. He protected himself from harm by convincing others of his greatness, and darn it if some little disease, and now some puny little prophet, was going to take that away.

Oh, sure, a disease was coursing through his body. But pride was coursing through his soul.

And Elisha knew it. If it had just been a skin disease that was Naaman's problem, I suspect Elisha would have come out, and in a few seconds would have taken care of the problem. But pride requires more than a doctor's cure. It requires a change in heart. It requires cooperation and obedience, and surrender by the one who is prideful. That takes more time.

Elisha knew that for this man to be healed and whole—I mean really whole—Naaman would need to learn humility.

The real lesson for us is that for many aspects of our lives—our relationships, our country, our world—the key to true healing is in the practice of true humility.

Now, *humility* is one of those interesting words that is so often misunderstood that we lose its essential meaning.

When I was growing up, I had a pretty distorted view of what it meant to be humble. I thought to be humble meant you thought of yourself as pretty lowly. It meant minimizing my own talents and abilities, not being proud of who I was or what I was able to do.

And it meant that I had to think of everyone else as better than me. For me, humility was the exact opposite of boasting. Rather than seeing myself as everything, I thought of myself as nothing.

I don't know if that meshes with your view of humility, but that is neither healthy nor biblical. Humility does not mean seeing yourself as nothing. It is not to be equated with low self-esteem or poor self-worth.

Instead, let's look at the word *humility* a little more closely. It comes from the Latin word *humus*, which literally means "dirt." Again, humility does not mean seeing ourselves as dirt, but it does mean seeing ourselves as grounded. Earthy. No better and no worse than the rest of all creation. It means acknowledging that you are connected to every other living creature on earth, and you are as dependent on others as they are on you. You cannot claim to be better than anyone else, because you depend on others. And you are no worse than anyone else, because others depend on you.

Here's another way of looking at it. Try remembering this. You are never as bad or as good as you think you are, and you are never as bad or as good as other people might say you are.

True humility is the gift of seeing yourself the way God sees you, and seeing yourself as part of an interconnected dependence on the lives of people with you and around you.

And if that's true, if that's the lesson that Naaman needed to hear and the true prescription for his deeper disease, then what about you and me? What difference would this kind of humility make for us today?

If you are in a broken relationship, in your marriage or your family, wouldn't a little dose of humility from you and from the other person go a long way in bringing healing?

Wouldn't a little more humility in your career transform the way you treat the people you work with and work for? Wouldn't it transform your values and the goals you set for your job?

Wouldn't a little more humility in our political systems, particularly in our political campaigns, go a long way to transforming the kind of polarizing rhetoric that divides our country?

Wouldn't a little more humility between countries and leaders of nations remind all of us of our interconnected dependence on one another? Wouldn't that transform international policies and even stem the brutal cycles of violence and war?

Wouldn't a little more humility between churches, denominations, and even faiths go a long way to healing the divisions that have brought incalculable harm to people of faith and to innocent people who have suffered because of religious competition?

In the end, Naaman took a bath. He followed Elisha's prescription, swallowed his pride, jumped in the river seven times, and emerged from that seventh soak clean and free. He was healed not just of the boils and lesions on his skin, but also from his arrogance, his addiction to power, and his need for others to affirm him.

Humility healed him. And Humpty Dumpty became whole again.

How about you?

The Wooden Miracle
2 Kings 6:1-7

The banks of the Jordan River had turned into a lumber mill. A large group of prophets, servants of Elisha, had exchanged their

FINDING HOPE IN HARD TIMES

How have you often thought of humility?

What has caused you to see yourself as either too high or too low in relation to other people?

What difference might it make for you to see yourself as interconnected and interdependent with others, even others who are different from you?

tunics and walking sticks for saws and axes. They were in rapid expansion mode, outgrowing their modest old boarding school, and were building some bigger digs for their new headquarters.

One by one, the trees along the Jordan fell, to be processed into construction material for their new home. We can imagine the pounding, grunting, and sawing, with the occasional boom of timber crashing to the ground.

And then, a piercing shriek in the air.

One of the men lost his axe head. Probably flew right off the handle in mid-swing. It's lucky it didn't land on a coworker. But for this particular prophet-turned-lumberjack, the moment felt just as bad. The axe head flew into the Jordan River, sinking somewhere into its murky depths.

It was a tough moment because of what it would mean for this man. It was a borrowed axe, and its owner would be expecting a full return of his tool, in the condition that he lent it. An axe was not something all that easy to come by—there were no hardware stores or big-box home improvement stores. If you wanted to own an axe, you had to forge one yourself or know someone who could make one for you. Iron would have been a precious commodity, as were the skills involved in turning it into something useful.

This prophet didn't just lose an axe. He lost someone's precious investment, and the trust involved in allowing him to borrow it.

This is all to say that when the prophet heard the sploosh of the water, his heart sank faster than the axe head. He was in trouble.

Elisha, serving as the ad hoc foreman of the operation, heard the man's panic and came over, asking the natural question. "Where did it fall?" Any of us who are parents can hear ourselves asking the same question of our kids who have lost something important, on the verge of tears, begging you for help. "Where did you see it last?" we ask them, each time realizing that if they *knew* the answer to that question, they wouldn't be panicking in the first place.

The man pointed to the general direction. Somewhere over there, gesturing toward the river. Over there, buried in the muddy river bottom by now, far too deep for us to suspend the work of all the men to do a search-and-rescue operation in the brisk Jordan current.

We might wonder at this point what was going on in Elisha's mind at that moment. Was he thinking about going in there himself? Was he going to order the man to switch into swim trunks and a snorkel and go dive for it until he found it? Might he even have considered reporting the axe lost, and bracing for the response of its sure-to-be-angry owner?

Whatever crossed his mind at that moment, Elisha emerged with steely resolve to find the axe head, and an ingenious plan to retrieve it.

To lift up that which was buried, to find that which was lost, would require a special kind of wood.

Verse 6 says that Elisha cut a piece of wood. We might imagine that he went over to some random, inconspicuous branch that was lying by the riverside, leftover fallout from a tree that had hit the ground. Maybe a piece that was largely ignored by everyone else. But Elisha saw purpose in it.

He cut the wood, but we're not told with what, or into what. We don't know what shape or what form it took, only that it needed cutting down to size. And when he threw that wood into the river, out into the general direction of the splash that the man heard, the miracle occurred. The buried rose again. The lost was found.

This is an odd story, isn't it? There aren't many other stories like it in the Bible, let alone in biographies of the prophets. And this is a story that is uniquely Elisha's. Whereas many of his episodes are echoes of similar vignettes featuring his predecessor, Elijah never had a story like this. Not a single story of something lost being found by a piece of wood.

So what do we make of this tale? How might we see some deeper truth in the grand scheme of the Christian story?

Well, for starters, what if we imagined—and, granted, this is sheer imagination—that the shape of the wood that Elisha cut . . . was a cross?

I'm not suggesting that he did use the shape of a cross, of course. But through the lens of our Christian convictions, as we allow this story to resonate with the whole of the story of salvation in Jesus, we might see here a foretaste of the gospel and the work of Jesus for us. Again, as that saying goes, "History doesn't repeat itself, but it does echo."

We might imagine that the idea of Elisha using a piece of wood to raise up something lost into new life can echo with the act of God using the cross. You and I, lost to our sin, sinking into the depths of a darkness of our own making, panicking as we acknowledge that our fate is ultimately on borrowed time, have been saved by a God who came down to earth in the form of a servant, "obedient to the point of death, even death on a cross" (Philippians 2:7-8).

Generations later, in that very same river, a thirty-year-old Palestinian named Jesus would arrive on that shoreline, face-to-face with a different kind of prophet. He would turn to John the Baptist, and together they would go down into the murky depths of the Jordan River. Jesus would sink below the water's surface like an axe head, and then rise, blinking and watery-eyed, looking up to heavens that had opened up like a curtain rising in a grand theater. A dove would descend on him, a part of himself, a Spirit reuniting with a Word, and he would hear the voice that would resonate in his ears until he would assume that cross for himself someday:

"You are my Son, the Beloved; with you I am well pleased" (Mark 1:11 NRSV).

If you have ever been baptized, this is your story, too. God's grace has been at work in your life since even before you recognized it, luring you and drawing you into a saving knowledge of God's love for you. Over time, that grace leads us to an acknowledgment that we cannot save ourselves. We need the work of Jesus to plunge into the depths of our heartache and brokenness and raise us up to new life and possibility. We cannot do it alone.

One night, during a fellowship dinner at my church, I was visiting parishioners at various tables. I stopped at the table of a woman named Sandra, who told me that in a few days, she was going to the hospital for a high-risk surgery on her brain. We chatted for a while about what she was feeling, about the concerns she had about the procedure and the recovery. We talked about what might go wrong and about what might happen if it did. She shared with me that while she was in a place of general peace about what would happen, and that her faith in God would be strong enough to sustain her, she did want to ask me for a favor.

"Sure," I said. "Anything."

"Would you mind helping me remember my baptism?" she asked.

I was deeply moved. "Of course," I said. I went into the kitchen and returned with a simple bowl of water. I sat next to her at the table, the sounds of eating, drinking, and conversation humming from tables all around us, and we bowed for a prayer. I recited the baptism liturgy the best I could, sharing with her the reminder of how God has used the symbol of water throughout history to demonstrate God's presence and power.

And then, I asked her to touch that water, remembering that she was a baptized, claimed, called, and loved child of God. She touched it with her fingers, and then on her forehead made the sign of a cross.

I remember thinking afterwards that only in the context of Christian community could she learn such vocabulary as the remembrance of baptism and draw such meaning from it in her time of need. Only in the story of her own salvation could she find echoes of a God who has always retrieved people from hopelessness with surprising acts of grace.

She made it through her surgery just fine, as it turns out. But more than her body receiving healing, she discovered something else. Her spirit, lost in fear and dread, had been found.

No, iron isn't supposed to float. Dead things are supposed to stay dead. And darkness can feel too heavy for light to break through. But God has a way of surprising us. God goes to any lengths necessary to find us, retrieve us, raise us up, and bring us home.

Opening Our Eyes to Hope
2 Kings 6:8-23

It has taken us until the very last story of this thrilling journey to discover that Elisha had a secret ability that no one knew about. He had super-hearing, which came in handy when the ruler of a nearby army was plotting to sweep in and destroy him and his people.

FINDING HOPE
IN HARD TIMES

If you have been baptized, how often do you think about what that baptism means?

What difference would it make in your life to remember that Jesus Christ has plunged into the depths of your sin and suffering and raised you to new life and possibility?

How might you remember your own baptism with gratitude?

The Arameans were no friend to the Israelites, which we already know from the story of Naaman. They had some power through generals like Naaman and the horses and chariots they commanded. And they had their target set on the people of God. The king of Aram gathered his generals together in their war room, laid out a big map, and I imagine they took out some of those little flags on those tiny flag stands. Then he thumped one squarely on a patch of land between them and the Israelites. It must have been a well-known place, like a trade route or a transportation thoroughfare, because the king of Aram considered it likely that the Israelites would pass through there soon. That was where he would set up camp and wait for them. Except somehow, Elisha was listening. He became a fly on the wall in the Aramean Pentagon, and he promptly brought his reconnaissance back to his king. *Don't go through there, king. Bad stuff will happen if you do.*

I'm not sure why the historian who chronicled these stories waited until now to tell us that Elisha had such strong hearing. But we find out here that Elisha has had this ability all along. "Time after time, Elisha warned the king, and the king stayed on the alert" (2 Kings 6:10).

I'm sure you and I would love to have an asset like that, someone who could advise us all the time about potential threats and pitfalls. That would be nice. Someone who could return from the field and say, "I've surveyed the possible options, and this course is the best one for you." Someone who could reassure you when you are frightened, challenge you when you are too comfortable, and prompt you to action when you feel paralyzed by indecision.

I'm not suggesting that Elisha is a foreshadowing of the Holy Spirit. But I am suggesting that the same God who sent prophets to guide kings in times of distress is the same God who gives you an advocate, a counselor, an advanced scout returning from the horizon, to give you the guidance and wisdom you need even when you don't think you do.

The Israelite king received Elisha's guidance and acted accordingly. He ordered his army to bypass the targeted area, sending the Aramean king into an absolute frenzy. "Curses! Foiled again!" we might imagine him mumbling, like a cartoon villain. Except this time, it was no laughing matter. He became resolved to find out who was the snitch or the spy or whatever it was that telegraphed his plans to the enemy.

And when he found out it was Elisha, he immediately picked up that little map flag that was standing on the spot of the failed ambush and slammed it down on Dothan, Elisha's hometown, right on top of his house. He sent a battalion of horses and chariots there, a monstrous force designed to sweep in, wipe out, and move on in a flash.

We're not told if Elisha was able to hear *these* plans. All we know is that the next morning, Elisha's servant walked outside and blinked in disbelief. All around him, in a giant, looming, threatening circle, he saw the Aramean army surrounding them, chomping at the bit for a single command by the general to commence their destruction. He rushed back into the house and said to Elisha words that were as natural a response as anything you and I would have said in the moment: "Oh, no! Master, what will we do?" (2 Kings 6:15).

I don't know if you've ever felt that way. It's likely that you have. You wake up in the morning, thinking about the possible outcomes of the day, and a feeling anywhere from nervousness to dread fills your spirit. I've sure been there. Before the sun is fully up and your eyes are rid of the sting of sleep, your mind is racing with thoughts that you cannot tame and scenarios you cannot control. It's all you can do to push yourself out of bed, when everything inside you wants to succumb to the gravitational pull of worry.

It's in these moments, and many like them, that we would do well to hear these words of Elisha. The words are not original to him, and are often repeated by many messengers throughout the Bible. It's a phrase that occurs so often in the Scriptures that it's surprising that we forget to apply it as often as we should. But unlike Elisha, we have imperfect hearing. And we need this reminder from God every now and then:

"Don't be afraid."

And then what he says is just downright puzzling: "because there are more of us than there are of them" (2 Kings 6:16).

It's at this point that even the most loyal servant of Elisha would understandably wonder if Elisha was delusional. The servant could see the evidence and do the math. A huge crowd of them, very few of us. A big mob of people with chariots, armor, and weapons, and a cozy little village of peons and prophets. A bunch, versus a bit.

C'mon, Elisha, you've got to be kidding.

But just like we are only now learning that Elisha has superhuman hearing, it turns out that this messenger from God also has superhuman eyesight. He has the ability to see with the eyes of God that which the eyes of human beings too readily miss. Elisha possesses the capacity to see a future that flies against the face of the evidence, a reality that is easy to overlook, but indisputable.

He could see that at anytime, anywhere, in any situation, God was with them. And that was enough.

So, Elisha prayed to God, and prayed a remarkable prayer. He prayed that at least for a moment, God would transfer his ability to see over to his servant. To open the servant's eyes to possibilities that Elisha knew were at play. "I pray that the eyes of your heart will have enough light to see what is the hope of God's call," Paul writes in Ephesians 1:18-19, "what is the richness of God's glorious inheritance among believers, and what is the overwhelming greatness of God's power that is working among us believers. This power is conferred by the energy of God's powerful strength."

And when you do open your eyes, when you do see that God, after all, is surrounding you with more love, guidance, care, and wisdom than you ever thought possible, then all of those fears about an uncertain future give way to a hope that is audacious, daring, and beautiful.

You may feel surrounded, but you are surrounded by God, as songwriter Michael W. Smith wrote in his song "Surrounded."

And it was enough. Elisha's servant saw then that the mountains around them were full of fiery chariots and horses. Elisha prayed a second prayer to God, that the Aramean army would be temporarily blinded and bewildered by their surroundings, such that they could be led to a different little flag on their map. With the power of God blindfolding them, Elisha escorted the army out of Dothan and about ten miles away to Samaria, right in the heart of Israel. And when they entered the city, Elisha asked God to take off their blinders, and immediately they noticed that they were no longer encamped around Dothan, no longer with the sizable advantage in numbers they thought they had. Instead, they were the ones under siege, caught without hope of escape, and fearing for their lives.

It's at this point that we would reasonably assume that the Arameans were going to meet their fate—just like the prophets of Baal did when Elijah beat them on Mount Carmel or like Ahab's family did when Jehu enacted the vengeance Elijah had predicted. We would anticipate that these Arameans, dead set on bringing death, would be killed on the spot as well.

But this story has one more surprise for us. As important as it is for us to hear Elisha's words to not fear when the enemy is surrounding us, it is just as critical for us to hear him tell the king of Israel that mercy, compassion, and love must overrule our impulses for hatred and violence.

Do not kill them, Elisha tells the king. Instead, feed them. Give them water. And send them away. And that's what the king of Israel did. He threw a banquet for them, in fact. A party, *for them*. It must have shocked them to their core, stunned their sensibilities. These soldiers, who had come prepared to kill and destroy, were being shown a kind of compassion they were not at all expecting.

And it was enough to transform their lives forever. It was the power of love. And from that moment on, they were enemies no more. They would never again attack the Israelites.

In 2017, a gathering of white supremacists made news around the world in a march called "Unite the Right" in Charlottesville, Virginia. For many of us, it was the largest gathering of hatred we have seen in our lifetimes.

Among them was a man named Ken Parker, a high-ranking official in the KKK, spewing hatred of people of color, Jews, and gay people. At the end of the rally, worn out from heat exhaustion and dehydration, he was doubled over in pain when he met a woman named Deeyah Khan. Deeyah is a Norwegian British documentary filmmaker of Punjabi descent, and she was there to chronicle the event. She saw Ken's physical pain and approached him, asking if he was okay and if there was anything she could do to ease his discomfort.

That little act alone planted a little seed of doubt in Ken's mind.

In an interview with NBC News, Ken said, "She was completely respectful to me and my fiancée the whole time. And so that kind of got me thinking: She's a really nice lady. Just because she's got darker skin and believes in a different god than the god I believe in, why am I hating these people?"[*]

On the Sunday of Charlottesville, I preached a sermon based on the encounter between Jesus and Nicodemus, where our congregation dared to pray for modern-day Nicodemuses, people among the white supremacists who might come to see the way of love instead of hate, just like Nicodemus did.

Six months after that weekend, Ken Parker, still nurturing the seeds of doubt planted by that filmmaker that day, noticed some African-American neighbors having a cookout in his apartment complex in Jacksonville, Florida. He and his fiancée approached them, and they began having a conversation. They were cordial with each other. They asked questions. They listened. They really listened.

He didn't know it at the time, but the black man was a pastor, Rev. William McKinnon III, of All Saints Holiness Church in Jacksonville. That night would be the first of many conversations they would share with each other.

---

[*] Aaron Franco and Morgan Radford, "Ex-KKK Member Denounces Hate Groups One Year after Rallying in Charlottesville," NBC News, August 10, 2018, https://www.nbcnews.com/news/us-news/ex-kkk-member-denounces-hate-groups-one-year-after-rallying-n899326.

"God was working on his heart when he came to the table that day, it was divine," said Pastor McKinnon, in an interview with the local Jacksonville news.[*]

And then later, just seven months after Charlottesville, Rev. McKinnon invited Ken and his girlfriend to church. In an Easter morning service, in a historically black congregation, the two of them worshiped.

A change was happening in Ken's life. A month later, Pastor McKinnon asked him to stand up before that congregation and give his testimony.

"I said I was a grand dragon of the KKK, and then the Klan wasn't hateful enough for me, so I decided to become a Nazi—and a lot of [the people in the church], their jaws about hit the floor and their eyes got real big. . . . But after the service, not a single one of them had anything negative to say. They're all coming up and hugging me and shaking my hand, you know, building me up instead of tearing me down."[†]

He had experienced the power of love through a community of people committed to the love of God—people who knew what it meant to be angry at injustice, but who also knew how to be angry without sinning.

Ken Parker looked at his skin and saw the visible signs of his hatred, the tattoos that revealed a Nazi symbol and the words "white pride." He has since had them removed through laser surgery.

But the biggest change is in the inside.

---

[*] Kenneth Amaro, "'Love Covers All' Says the Pastor of Former Neo Nazi Ken Parker," *First Coast News*, August 10, 2018, https://www.firstcoastnews.com/article/news/love-covers-all-says-the-pastor-of-former-neo-nazi-ken-parker/77-582483371.

[†] Franco and Radford, "Ex-KKK Member Denounces Hate Groups."

Just a few months after giving his testimony in that church, he traded in his old KKK robes for a white robe of baptism. Walking hand in hand into the water with Rev. William McKinnon, he experienced the waters of baptism and the grace of God's forgiveness.

In the NBC News segment, Ken said, "I want to say I'm sorry. I do apologize.... I know I've spread hate and discontent through this city immensely—probably made little kids scared to sleep in their own beds in their own neighborhoods." And now he has a message for white supremacists. "You can definitely get out of this movement. I mean, I was into that so much—it was my life, for six years. I never thought I would get out.... Get out. You're throwing your life away."*

Ken Parker is an answer to the prayers of any of us who prayed like Elisha, that people's eyes would be opened to the reality of God's love all around us. And despite our most human instincts to hate and divide, God calls us to have the compassion of Elisha, to extend a hand of hospitality instead of a weapon of destruction.

We might wonder: what if the documentary filmmaker Deeyah Khan had chosen to respond to the disgusting dehumanization of the KKK by dehumanizing Ken Parker? What if Rev. McKinnon and his congregation had chosen the easy way of hating Ken Parker?

Now, imagine what can happen when you and I choose to live in love, take the time, and watch our words. How many more Ken Parkers might God bring into the light?

As Pastor William McKinnon said, "It is clear to me that love covers all."[†]

---

* Franco and Radford, "Ex-KKK Member Denounces Hate Groups."
† Amaro, " 'Love Covers All.' "

FINDING HOPE
IN HARD TIMES

In what way do you feel surrounded by forces of suffering and anxiety that feel beyond your control?

How might God be calling you to open your eyes, realize God's presence all around you, and seek the way of compassion and love, rather than revenge and hatred?